jomo
knits

jomo
knits

21 PROJECTS TO CELEBRATE THE **JOY** OF MISSING OUT

Christine Boggis

THE GUILD OF MASTER CRAFTSMAN
PUBLICATIONS

First published 2019 by
Guild of Master Craftsman Publications Ltd
Castle Place, 166 High Street, Lewes,
East Sussex BN7 1XU

Text © Christine Boggis, 2019
Copyright in the Work © GMC Publications Ltd, 2019

ISBN 978 1 78494 505 3

While every effort has been made to obtain permission from the copyright holders for all material used in this book, the publishers will be pleased to hear from anyone who has not been appropriately acknowledged and to make the correction in future reprints.

The publishers and author can accept no legal responsibility for any consequences arising from the application of information, advice or instructions given in this publication.

A catalogue record for this book is available from the British Library.

Publisher Jonathan Bailey
Production Manager Jim Bulley
Senior Project Editor Virginia Brehaut
Editor Nicola Hodgson
Managing Art Editor Gilda Pacitti
Design Luana Gobbo
Photography Laurel Guilfoyle and Anthony Bailey

Colour origination by GMC Reprographics
Printed and bound in China

CONTENTS

Nest

Breakfast in bed
page 12

Rainy day
page 21

Shades of sheep
page 24

Explore

Just be me
page 46

Forest walk
page 55

Me-time
page 60

Share

Hearts and diamonds
page 81

Wrap it up
page 88

End of the rainbow
page 95

Fairy lights
page 29

Dip your toes
page 32

Box-set binge
page 36

I'm not biased
page 41

Cherish
page 65

Feel the rhythm
page 68

Switch off
page 73

I knit anywhere
page 74

Walking on rainbows
page 96

Warm heart
page 99

Lovely bobbly
page 102

Mittens dressed up as lamb *page 106*

*"For everything you have missed,
you have gained something else."*
RALPH WALDO EMERSON

What is JOMO?

A FEW YEARS AGO, a clever marketeer coined the acronym FOMO: fear of missing out. Ever since, companies have been leveraging our anxiety about what we might be missing out on to sell us everything from holidays and gig tickets to kitchen appliances and clothes.

FOMO fuelled, and was fuelled by, social media posts of people out having fun, eating photogenic dinners and jumping into swimming pools. But a time came when photos of all those people driven by FOMO to constant consumption, striving and activity started to feel exhausting. That was followed by the thought that it might be nice just to put on pyjamas and curl up in front of the TV with a box set, a cup of tea and a whole load of wool – even if that meant missing out on something ostensibly more exciting. With that idea, JOMO was born: the joy of missing out.

JOMO and crafting go together like needles and yarn, like Starsky and Hutch, like a cup of tea and a sit down. Knitting is not about fast fashion, getting into the latest trend and then getting rid of it when it's over. It's not about something that is here today and gone tomorrow that you might miss out on if you're not quick enough. It's not about buying into something. It's slower, softer and quieter than that.

JOMO is about making something slowly, so that you or someone you love can treasure it forever, or making for the sheer joy of making. It's about creating something that suits your body shape, whatever that may be. It's about fudging together something that might have a few mistakes but is perfect in its own way, or about knitting up and ripping back the same thing over and over again until it's exactly how you want it. It's about sitting at home content that, if you are missing out on something, it's not as good as what you're doing right now.

About this book

JOMO knitting is about making something slowly, although the knits in this book are actually quite quick. They are not as quick as going out and buying a cheap 100% acrylic jumper, but in knitting terms they're quite swift. Little projects such as the Me-time mitts (page 60) could be made by a fast knitter in an evening or two, and by a beginner in a week if you put your mind to it.

All the designs aim to be accessible to beginners but interesting enough for knitters of any level to enjoy. If you've never knitted before, the Fairy lights hat (page 29), Box-set binge blanket (page 36) or End of the rainbow baby blanket (page 95) could be good places to start. However, if you want to jump right in and knit a jumper for your first project, go ahead! It's probably not as hard as you think and you'll love it.

The designs in this book are knitted in beautiful chunky yarns, most with a high wool content. Many are knitted in the round, either from the bottom up or the top down, so circular needles are a must. I highly recommend learning the magic loop method (see page 128) – it's perfect for lazy or scatter-brained knitters who don't want to hunt down double-pointed needles in a range of sizes, and if your needle collection is small it means you only have to invest in one or two. Some designers swear by seamed garments – they say it gives the pieces structure – but these chunky designs have plenty of structure already and I hate sewing up, so in the round is the way I prefer.

SO WHAT IS JOMO KNITTING?

JOMO knitting is not being told what you should be doing with your time by marketeers or anyone else.

JOMO knitting is about slow fashion, spending time crafting something really special from beautiful materials to keep forever or give to someone who will cherish it.

JOMO knitting is about being a maker rather than a consumer.

JOMO knitting is knowing you're not missing out if your body shape is different from what we're told is the norm.

JOMO knitting is about being in the moment that is, not wishing for a different sort of moment that might look more impressive on a social media feed.

JOMO knitting is about embracing who you are and loving it – no matter what anyone else might think.

There's nothing better than snuggling up in your own space with yarn and needles and enjoying a quiet bit of me-time. Make your home a woolly haven with these knits designed for cocooning and comfort.

Nest

Breakfast in bed

This top-down, in-the-round jumper with pretty lace panels and trendy bishop sleeves is perfect for those days when you just want to stay home and snuggle up. The Cable Twist Lace pattern comes from Wendy Bernard's brilliant book, *The Knitting All Around Stitch Dictionary.*

Sizes

To fit bust: 32–34[36–38:40–42:44–46]in (81–86[91–97:102–107:112–117]cm)
Actual bust: 46[50½:55:59]in (117[128:140:150]cm)
Front length: 21¼in (54cm)
Back length: 24¾in (63cm)
Sleeve length: 16in (41cm)
Figures in square brackets refer to larger sizes. Where only one set of figures is given, this applies to all sizes.

You will need

Erika Knight Maxi Wool
   100% pure British wool
   (approx. 87yd/80m per 100g)
7[7:8:9] x 100g hanks in Storm
10mm (UK000:US15) circular needle
   40in (100cm) long
Set of 10mm (UK000:US15)
   double-pointed needles (optional)
11 stitch markers
Stitch holders or scrap yarn
NOTE: Yarn amounts are based on average requirements and are approximate.

Tension

9.5 sts and 13 rows to 4in (10cm) over st st.
One Cable Twist Lace pattern repeat (15 sts and 18 rounds) measures 6¼ x 5½in (16 x 14cm).
Use larger or smaller needles if necessary to obtain the correct tension.

Abbreviations

See page 148.

Pattern note

Stitch markers are used to denote the start and end of each round; the division between left back and left sleeve (m1); left sleeve and front (m2); front and right sleeve (m3); and right sleeve and right back (m4). Other markers may be used to denote the start and end of each pattern panel. These will not be numbered. Make sure you know which marker is which. Where markers are not mentioned, simply slip them.

I used shadow wrap short rows (see page 140) for the short row shaping.

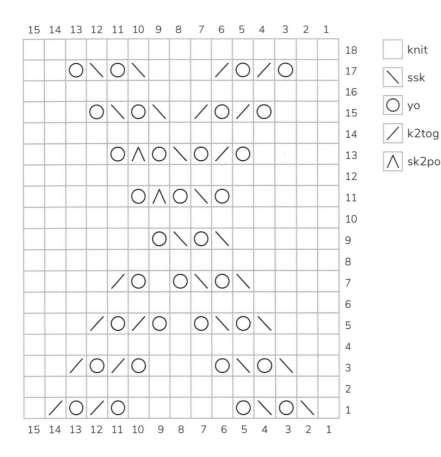

	knit
\	ssk
O	yo
/	k2tog
∧	sk2po

Jumper

With the circular needle, cast on 60 sts using the long tail method (see page 119). Using the magic loop method (see page 128), join to work in the round, taking care not to twist stitches, pm to mark beg of round at mid-back.

Round 1: (K1, p1) around. Rep round 1 five more times.

Next round (inc): Kfb, k to end (61 sts).

SHAPE BACK NECK

Set-up round: K13, pm1, k5, pm2, k25, pm3, k5, pm4, k13.

Short row 1: K to m2, sm, k2, w&t.

Short row 2: P back across start-of-round marker to m3, sm, p2, w&t.

Short row 3: K to m2, sm, k1, w&t.

Short row 4: P to m3, sm, p1, w&t.

Short row 5: K to end of round.

SET RAGLAN INCREASES AND LACE PANEL

NOTE: Read all this section before starting work: the whole increase pattern is detailed before the lace panel instructions are given, but both are worked at the same time.

Round 1 (inc): Knitting wraps tog

Cable Twist Lace pattern

Worked over 15 sts and 18 rounds.

Round 1: K1, (ssk, yo) twice, k5, (yo, k2tog) twice, k1.

Round 2 and all alt rounds: Knit.

Round 3: K2, (ssk, yo) twice, k3, (yo, k2tog) twice, k2.

Round 5: K3, (ssk, yo) twice, k1, (yo, k2tog) twice, k3.

Round 7: K4, (ssk, yo) twice, k1, yo, k2tog, k4.

Round 9: K5, (ssk, yo) twice, k6.

Round 11: K5, yo, ssk, yo, sk2po, yo, k5.

Round 13: K4, yo, k2tog, yo, ssk, yo, sk2po, yo, k4.

Round 15: K3, (yo, k2tog) twice, k1, (ssk, yo) twice, k3.

Round 17: K2, (yo, k2tog) twice, k3, (ssk, yo) twice, k2.

Rounds 1–18 form patt and are repeated.

with wrapped sts as you come to them, work as foll: *K to 1 st before marker, m1L, k1, sm, k1, m1R; rep from * four times, k to end (69 sts: 14 for Left back, 7 sts each Sleeve, 27 for Front, 14 for Right back).

Round 2: Knit.

SIZE 1 ONLY
Round 3: Knit.
Rep last 3 rounds 9 times (141 sts: 23 sts for each side of Back, 25 for each Sleeve and 45 for Front).

SIZES 2, 3 AND 4 ONLY
Rep last 2 rounds 3[9:13] times (93[141:173] sts).
Next round (inc): Rep inc round (101[149:181] sts).

SIZES 2 AND 3 ONLY
Knit 2 rounds.
Rep last 3 rounds 6[2] more times (149[165] sts).

ALL SIZES
Rep inc round 0[1:1:1] more time. 141[157:173:189] sts: 23[25:27:29] for each side of Back, 25[29:33:37] for each Sleeve and 45[49:53:57] for Front. After this round, divide body and sleeves.

AT THE SAME TIME set Cable Twist Lace patt as folls:

FRONT
Round 4: K to m2, sm, k7, pm, work row 1 of Cable Twist Lace patt, pm, k to end.
This round sets position of Cable Twist Lace patt on front. Cont in patt throughout.

SLEEVES
Round 16: K to m1, sm, k2, pm, work row 1 of Cable Twist Lace patt, pm, patt to m3, k2, pm, work row 1 of Cable Twist Lace patt, pm, k to end.
This round sets position of Cable Twist Lace patt on sleeves. Cont in patt throughout.

DIVIDE BODY AND SLEEVES
Next round: K to m1, remove m, slip sleeve sts to scrap yarn, using knitted-on method (see page 120) cast on 10[10:12:12] sts, pm after 5th[5th:6th:6th] cast-on st, remove m2, patt to m3, remove marker, slip sleeve sts to scrap yarn, using knitted-on method cast on 10[10:12:12] sts, pm after

5th[5th:6th:6th] cast-on st, remove m4, k to end. 109[119:131:139] sts: 27[30:33:35] for each side of Back and 55[59:65:69] for Front.

TIP: Make a note of which row of the lace pattern you are on for the sleeves so that it is easier to pick up when you come back to them.

Body
Cont in patt as set, slipping markers, until a total of 3 full reps of Cable Twist Lace patt have been worked.

SHAPE BACK HEM
Short row 1: K28, w&t.
Short row 2: P to end of round, p28, w&t.
Short row 3: K to last st before wrapped st, w&t.
Short row 4: P to last st before wrapped st, w&t.
Rep rows 3 and 4 once more, then k to end of round.
Next round: K2tog, knit to end (108[118:130:138] sts).
Next round: (K1, p1) around.

Rep last round 5 more times.
Cast off in rib.

Sleeves (both alike)

Slip Sleeve sts from scrap yarn back to needle, then pick up and knit 1 st in gap between Sleeve sts and underarm cast-on, 10[10:12:12] sts across underarm cast-on of Body and 1 st in gap between cast-on and Sleeve sts. Pm after 6th[6th:7th:7th] picked-up st (37[41:47:51] sts). Cont straight in patt as set in yoke for 28[20:8:0] rounds.

SHAPE SLEEVE

Next round (dec): K2tog, patt to end (36[40:46:50] sts). Patt 3 rounds.

Next round (dec): K1, k2tog, patt to last 3 sts, ssk, k1 (34[38:44:48] sts). Rep last 4 rounds 1[3:6:8] times (32 sts). Patt 1 round – row 18 of Cable Lace Twist patt. Knit 2 rounds.

SHAPE BISHOP SLEEVE

Next round (dec): K1, k3tog, k to last 4 sts, sk2po, k1 (28 sts). **Next round:** Knit. **Next round (dec):** Rep dec round above (24 sts). **Next round:** (K1, p1) around. Rep last round 7 more times. Cast off in rib.

To finish

Weave in ends neatly. Pin to measurements, cover with damp cloths and leave to dry.

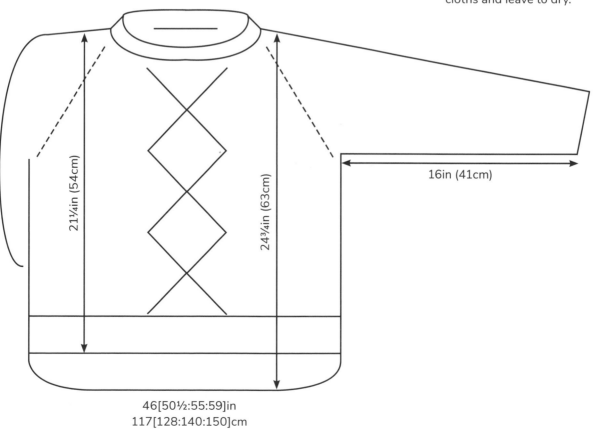

21¼in (54cm)

24¾in (63cm)

16in (41cm)

46[50½:55:59]in
117[128:140:150]cm

Rainy day

This super-simple, super-cosy cardigan is knitted from side to side in a basic rectangle with armholes. The sleeves are then picked up and knitted to the length you want. The name of the garment was inspired by the yarn itself – the flowing, puddling colours look like water even before they are knitted up into garter stitch bumps that resemble raindrops.

Size
To fit: Average adult
Width edge to edge:
    Approx. 53¼in (135cm)
Length: Approx. 27½in (70cm)
Sleeve length: 19¾in (50cm)
Note: This fabric is very stretchy,
    so the measurements are
    approximate.

You will need
Malabrigo Rasta 100% kettle-dyed
    pure Merino wool
    (approx. 90yd/82m per 150g)
8 x 150g hanks in 856 Azules
15mm (UK–:US19) needles
Stitch marker
Shawl stick or giant safety pin
    (optional)
Note: Yarn amounts given are
based on average requirements
and are approximate.

Tension
7 sts and 9 rows to 4in (10cm).
Use larger or smaller needles
if necessary to obtain the
correct tension.

Abbreviations
See page 148.

Body
(worked from edge to edge)
Cast on 52 sts.
Row 1 (RS): Purl.
Row 2: Knit.
SET MAIN PATTERN
Row 1 (RS): Knit.
Row 2: P2, k to last 2 sts, p2.
Rep rows 1 and 2 until piece
measures approx. 15¾in (40cm),
ending with a WS row.

SHAPE ARMHOLES
*Row 1 (RS): K8, cast off 16,
k to end.
Row 2: P2, k26, cast on 16,
k to last 2 sts, p2.*
Cont in main patt until piece
measures approx. 37½in (95cm),
ending with a WS row.
Rep from * to * to shape second
armhole.
Cont in main patt until piece
measures approx. 52¼in (133cm),
ending with a WS row.
Next row (RS): Purl.
Next row: Knit.
Cast off loosely.

Sleeves (both alike)
With RS facing, starting at
underarm, pick up and knit 1 st
at underarm, 16 sts up one side of
armhole, 2 sts at shoulder, 16 sts
down other side of armhole and
1 more st at underarm (36 sts).
Pm to mark beg of round.
Round 1: Purl.
Round 2: Knit.
Rep rounds 1 and 2 three more
times, then round 1 again.
SET DECREASE PATTERN
Round 1 (dec): K1, k2tog, k to last
3 sts, ssk, k1 (34 sts).
Rounds 2 and 4: Purl.
Round 3: Knit.
Rep these 4 rounds 2 more times
(30 sts), then dec every alt round
until you have 16 sts, ending with
last dec round.
Next round: (K1, p1) around.
Rep this round 13 more times.
Cast off in rib.

To finish

Weave in ends neatly. Pin to measurements, cover with damp cloths and leave to dry. Fasten with a shawl stick (pictured right) or a giant safety pin, or sew on buttons if you wish. As this fabric is quite loose and drapey, you could use buttons that will fit through the existing gaps in the fabric, or you could crochet a short chain to make a button loop and attach this to accommodate a large statement button.

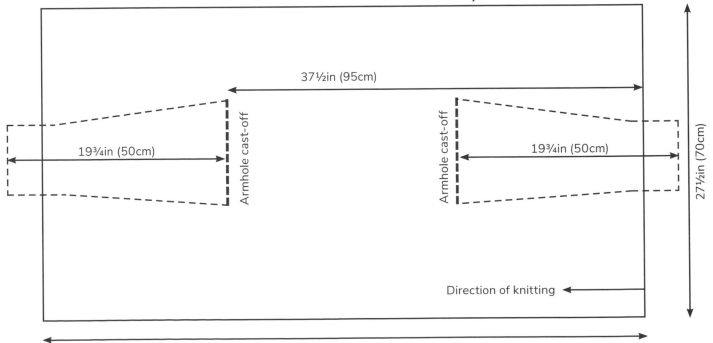

37½in (95cm)

Armhole cast-off

19¾in (50cm)

Armhole cast-off

19¾in (50cm)

27½in (70cm)

Direction of knitting

53¼in (135cm)

Shades of sheep

I love the natural shades of sheep, from the black sheep of the nursery rhyme to soft and creamy whites. Yorkshire wool shop Baa Ram Ewe's gorgeous Dovestone Natural Chunky sheep shades make the perfect gradient for a simple triangle shawl.

Size
To fit: Anyone
Wingspan: Approx. 71in (180cm)
Length: Approx. 39½in (100cm)

You will need
Baa Ram Ewe Dovestone Natural
    Chunky 100% British wool
    (approx. 131yd/120m per 100g)
1 x 100g ball each in shades 1 (A),
    2 (B) and 3 (C)
2 x 100g balls each in shades 4 (D)
    and 5 (E)
7mm (UK2:US10½) circular needle
    59in (150cm) long
2 stitch markers
Note: Yarn amounts given are based
on average requirements and are
approximate.

Tension
Tension is not critical to this project.

Abbreviations
See page 148.

Pattern note
This shawl is started with a
garter-stitch tab cast on. For full
instructions on this technique,
see page 120.

Shawl

GARTER STITCH TAB CAST ON

Using A, cast on 3 sts.

Knit 5 rows.

Turn piece 90 degrees clockwise, pick up and k3 sts along side edge (1 in each g st bump).

Turn work 90 degrees clockwise again, pick up and k3 sts along cast-on edge (9 sts).

SET GARTER STITCH INCREASE PATTERN

Set-up row 1: K3, yo, pm, k3, pm, yo, k3 (11 sts).

Set-up row 2: Knit.

Row 1: K3, yo, k to m, yo, sm, k3, sm, yo, k to last 3 sts, yo, k3 (inc 4).

Row 2: Knit.

Rep rows 1 and 2 until you have 99 sts, ending on a WS row.

SET DILUTED STRIPES PATTERN

Join B but do not break A.

Row 1 (RS): Using B, k3, yo, k to m, yo, sm, k3, sm, yo, k to last 3 sts, yo, k3 (inc 4). Slide sts back to other end of needle to work RS again.

Row 2 (RS): Using A, purl. Turn work.

Row 3 (WS): Using B, p3, yo, p to m, yo, sm, p3, sm, yo, p to last 3 sts, yo, p3 (inc 4). Slide sts back to other end of needle to work WS again.

Row 4 (WS): Using A, knit. Turn work.

Rep rows 1–4 two more times (123 sts).

Break A and cont in B only until you have 159 sts, ending on a WS row.

Work rows 1–4 of Diluted Stripes patt 3 times in total, but using C and B in place of B and A (183 sts).

Break B and cont in C only until you have 203 sts, ending on a WS row.

Work rows 1–4 of Diluted Stripes patt 3 times in total, but using D and C in place of B and A (227 sts).

Break C and cont in D only until you have 243 sts, ending on a WS row.

Work rows 1–4 of Diluted Stripes patt 3 times in total, but using E and D in place of B and A (267 sts).

Break D and cont in E only until you have 279 sts, ending on a WS row.

SET EDGE PATTERN

Next row (RS): K3, yo, k1, (yo, k2tog) to m, yo, sm, k3, sm, yo, (ssk, yo) to last 4 sts, k1, yo, k3 (283 sts).

Next row: Knit.

Next row (inc): K3, m1L, k to m, m1R, sm, k3, sm, m1L, k to last 3 sts, m1R, k3 (287 sts).

Rep last 2 rows 1 more time (291 sts).

Knit 1 row.

Cast off loosely.

To finish

Weave in ends neatly. Pin to measurements, cover with damp cloths and leave to dry.

Fairy lights

This super-soft Merino beanie is as cosy and comforting as a window full of fairy lights on a dark and dreary day – and it's just as beautiful, with different colours popping up in each purl bump like shiny jewels. On top of that, it's extremely quick and easy to make – so knit it up quickly, slip it on and stay warm.

Size

To fit: Average adult
Circumference:
    Approx. 21¼in (54cm)
Depth: Approx. 9¾in (25cm)
Note: This fabric is very stretchy,
    so the measurements are
    approximate.

You will need

Malabrigo Rasta 100% kettle-dyed
    pure Merino wool
    (approx. 90yd/82m per 150g)
1 x 150g hanks in 5 Aniversario
15mm (UK–:US19) double-pointed
    or circular needles
Stitch marker
Note: Yarn amounts given are based
on average requirements and are
approximate.

Tension

6 sts and 11 rounds to 4in (10cm).
Use larger or smaller needles
if necessary to obtain the
correct tension.

Abbreviations

See page 148.

Hat

Cast on 32 sts. Join to work in the round, taking care not to twist stitches, pm to mark start of round.
Rib round: (K2, p2) around.
Rep this round once more.
*Knit 4 rounds.
Purl 4 rounds.
Rep from * once more.
Knit 4 rounds.

SHAPE CROWN

Round 1: (K4, k2tog) to last 2 sts, k2 (27 sts).
Round 2: (K3, k2tog) to last 2 sts, k2 (22 sts).
Round 3: (K2, k2tog) to last 2 sts, k2 (17 sts).
Round 4: (K1, k2tog) to last 2 sts, k2 (12 sts).
Round 5: (K2tog) around (6 sts).
Break yarn, thread through rem 6 sts and pull tight to fasten off.

To finish

Weave in ends neatly. Block
if required.

An introduction to modern kniterature

For me, there's nothing more luxurious than a long lie-in with a good book. I'm a bookworm, and if I have any leisure time that's not devoted to knitting you'll find me reading.

As a busy working mum I have to multi-task, so I've experimented with combining my two passions. There are two ways to do that. Option one is to knit while reading. This is possible but challenging.

First, you need the right knitting project. Something very simple that you don't have to look at or think about is ideal – a stocking-stitch sock, or plain sleeves, like the

"The high value put upon every minute of time, the idea of hurry-hurry as the most important objective of living, is unquestionably the most dangerous enemy of joy."

HERMANN HESSE

NON-FICTION

The Curse of the Boyfriend Sweater: Essays on Crafting
by Alanna Okun (Flatiron Books)

This lovely memoir of a young woman's life, love and crafts had me laughing, crying and quoting it before I'd got past page 15. Funny, moving and instructional, it intersperses Manhattan-based writer Alanna's life story with her crafting experiences and light-hearted lists of things she's learned over the years.

FICTION

The Friday Night Knitting Club
by Kate Jacobs (Hodder)

Set in cosy knitting shop Walker & Daughter in New York's Upper West Side, this touching novel tells the story of single mum Georgia Walker, her young daughter Dakota, their grandmotherly friend Anita and their pals in the shop's Friday Night Knitting Club. Perfect comfort reading.

Knit One, Kill Two
by Maggie Sefton (Berkley Books)

The first in a series of 15 mysteries, this novel tells the story of lonely accountant Kelly Flynn, who returns to her hometown in Colorado after her beloved Aunt Helen dies. She finds a ready-made group of friends in nearby idyllic yarn shop House of Lambspun. They support her through her grief, initiate her into the wonderful world of knitting and even help her solve a murder mystery.

Unravelled
by Robyn Harding (Berkley Books)

This crafty chick-lit read involves freelance writer Beth Carruthers, who joins a Seattle Stitch and Bitch club in a bid to meet new people after breaking up with her commitment-phobic boyfriend of four years. Learning the craft, she meets a new group of friends who help her rebuild her social life.

ones for the Wrap it up cardigan (see page 88). Second, you need the right book. Really chunky paperbacks won't work because it's hard to keep them open on the right page, so go for a slimmer volume or a medium-sized hardback. Tiny print will be a bother: you will have to look at your knitting from time to time and don't want to get lost each time you do.

The best option to start with could be a large-print hardback, even if you don't normally need to read large-print books. These can be wedged open with something small but heavy, like a mobile phone or a stone.

If that sounds too tricky (or unnecessary), try option two: reading about knitting. The past few years have seen a great collection of fiction and non-fiction books about the craft appear. Here is a selection of my favourites.

Dip your toes

There's nothing like pure wool to keep you toasty – which is vital in the Shetland Islands, where this wool comes from. Tapping into the trend for dip-dyeing, these socks show off two complementary shades in a simple cable pattern.

Size

To fit: Average woman's feet

Cuff circumference: 8in (20cm) (stretchy)

Foot length: 9¾in (24.5cm) (adjustable)

You will need

West Yorkshire Spinners The Croft 100% Shetland Island wool (approx. 182yd/166m per 100g)

1 x 100g hank in 754 Heylor (A)

1 x 100g hank in 760 Dalsetter (B)

5mm (UK6:US8) double-pointed or circular needles

Cable needle

Stitch holder

Stitch markers

Note: Yarn amounts given are based on average requirements and are approximate.

Tension

17 sts and 23 rounds to 4in (10cm) over st st.

One patt rep (20 sts and 6 rounds) measures approx. 3¼ x 1¼in (8 x 3.5cm). Use larger or smaller needles if necessary to obtain the correct tension.

Abbreviations

C3L = slip next st to cn and hold at front of work, k2, k1 from cn.

C3R = slip next 2 sts to cn and hold at back of work, k1, k2 from cn.

C4B = slip next 2 sts to cn and hold at back of work, k2, k2 from cn.

For standard abbreviations, see page 148.

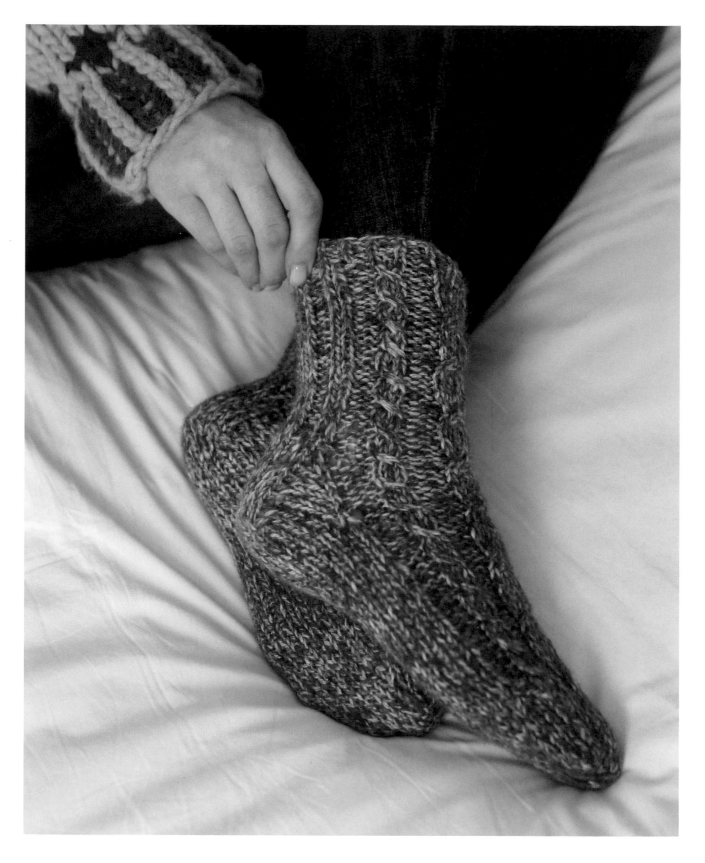

Sock (make 2)

Cast on 36 sts. Join to work in the round, taking care not to twist sts, and pm to mark beg of round.

Rib round: (K1, p1) around.
Rep rib round 3 more times.

SET LEG PATTERN

Rounds 1–3: (K2, p2) 4 times, k2, p2, k3, p2, k4, p2, k3, p2.

Round 4: (K2, p2) 4 times, k2, p2, C3L, p2, k4, p2, C3R, p2.

Rounds 5–7: As round 1.

Round 8: (K2, p2) 4 times, k2, p2, C3L, p2, C4B, p2, C3R, p2.

Rounds 1–8 form patt. Rep these 8 rounds twice more, then rounds 1–4 again.

Heel flap

Worked back and forth across first 18 sts only. You may wish to slip rem 18 sts for top of foot onto a stitch holder, but this is not essential.

Row 1: K18, turn.

Row 2 (WS): (Sl1, p1) to end.

Row 3 (RS): Sl1, k to end.

Rep rows 2 and 3 four more times until heel flap measures approx. 2in (5cm).

TURN HEEL

Still worked on 18 heel flap sts only.

Row 1 (WS): Sl1, p9, p2tog, p1, turn.

Row 2 (RS): Sl1, k3, ssk, k1, turn.

Row 3: Sl1, p4, p2tog, p1, turn.

Row 4: Sl1, k5, ssk, k1, turn.

Row 5: Sl1, p6, p2tog, p1, turn.

Row 6: Sl1, k7, ssk, k1, turn.

Row 7: Sl1, p8, p2tog, turn.

Row 8: Sl1, k8, ssk, turn (10 sts).

SHAPE HEEL GUSSET

Set-up round 1: Pick up and k9 sts along side of heel flap (1 in each slipped st and 1 more between side of heel and top of foot), pm1 (this will be beg of round), patt 18 across top of foot (row 5 of patt), pm2, pick up and k 9 sts along side of heel flap (1 between top of foot sts and side of heel and 1 in each slipped st), pm3, k across 9 sole sts (46 sts).

Set-up round 2: K tbl to m1, sm, patt to m2, sm, k tbl to m3, remove m3, k to end of round.

Dec round 1: Patt to m, sm, ssk, k to 2 sts before end-of-round m, k2tog (dec 2).

Dec round 2: Patt to m, sm, k to end.

Rep rounds 1 and 2 until 36 sts remain, ending with row 4 of patt. Patt 1 round as now set, with cable patt across top of foot and st st across sole (row 5 of patt).

CHANGE COLOUR

Break A and join B. Patt as set in B (row 6 of patt).

Cont in patt as now set in B to end of this patt rep and for 3 more full 8-row patt reps, then work rows 1 and 2 again.

Note: You can adjust the foot length at this point by knitting more or fewer rows, ending patt on row 4 or 8.

SHAPE TOE

Round 1 (dec): *K1, ssk, k12, k2tog, k1, pm; rep from * to end.

Round 2: Knit.

Round 3 (dec): *K1, ssk, k to 3 sts before m, k2tog, k1, sm; rep from * to end.

Rep rounds 2 and 3 twice more, then round 2 again.

Distribute toe sts evenly over two needles, then graft using Kitchener stitch (see page 138).

To finish

Weave in ends. Block if required.

5 ways to find more time for knitting

1

TAKE THE TRAIN

If you travel to work by train or bus, you could spend some of your time in transit knitting. More and more men and women are doing that to combat the stress of the daily commute.

2

LUNCH IS NOT FOR WIMPS

Do you take a lunch break? Research has shown that taking a break from work is good for our mental and physical wellbeing. We can work better if we come back refreshed from a brief rest than if we simply plough on through. Knitting is a great way to switch off from the stresses of your day job as you get a few more rows in.

3

TV TIME

If you're just starting out with knitting, you may not be able to take your eyes off your needles as you work, but as you become more proficient you will need to concentrate less. If you like watching TV, this can be a great combination with your hobby. When I was learning to knit I liked to listen to audio books (podcasts hadn't been invented then), but now I hardly ever watch TV without my knitting.

4

PARK LIFE

If you have children of a certain age, you may spend hours in the park while they play – and this is a great time to knit. Don't pick a complicated project that you have to follow carefully. You're bound to be interrupted, so a simple knit that you can pick up and put down without too much bother is perfect.

5

BEDTIME STITCHERY

Knitting can be incredibly soothing and a wonderful way to wind down after a tough or busy day. Working a few rows in bed just before turning the lights out is a great way to ground you in the moment and take time to think over, assess and release any lingering cares or worries from the day.

Box-set binge

This ultra-cosy blanket wants to be more than just a standard stocking stitch – so it's diverged into garter stitch as well. It's probably the simplest knit in this book and, if you put your mind to it, you can whip it up in the time it takes to watch two or three films or a short series.

Size
38½ x 70¾in (98 x 180cm)

You will need
Loopy Mango Big Loop 100% US Merino wool (approx. 125yd/115m per 1134g)
2 x 1134g balls in Grey Heather
25mm (UK–:US50) needles

Note: Yarn amounts are based on average requirements and are approximate. Yarn weights vary slightly between the US and Europe but this shouldn't affect the outcome.

Tension
2.5 sts and 3 rows to 4in (10cm) over st st.
Use larger or smaller needles if necessary to obtain the correct tension, although tension is not critical to this project.

Abbreviations
See page 148.

Pattern note
To join the two balls, use the wet-splicing method (see page 39).

Blanket
Cast on 24 sts.
Row 1: Knit.
Row 2: K12, p12.
Rep rows 1 and 2 until Blanket measures approx. 70¾in (180cm), ending with row 2.
Cast off.

To finish
Weave in ends using your fingers, then trim. Pin blanket to measurements, cover with damp cloths and leave to dry.

WET SPLICING

Wet splicing is a way of joining yarn ends with no waste or ends to weave in, so the join should be completely invisible. This method uses water and friction to felt two ends of yarn together into a single seamless strand.

1 Get the two ends of yarn and pull them apart a little so that you can see the separate fibres.

2 Sprinkle a small amount of water on both ends. Some people use saliva for this, but a glass of water is fine. The ends should be damp but not soaking wet.

3 Rub the two yarn ends together firmly between your hands. They will start to feel warm, which is good – it is the combination of heat and friction that will join them into one strand.

4 The end result is a seamless join.

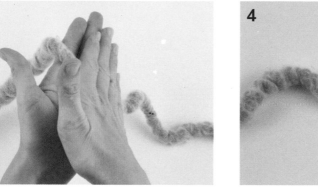

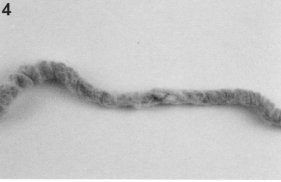

I'm not biased

Knitting on the bias is great fun: it's always changing, and it feels as if you're working diagonally. You start by increasing to the width you want, and end by decreasing back to nothing. I'm not biased, but I think it's brilliant.

Size

To fit: 16[20]in (40[50]cm) square
cushion pad when slightly
stretched

Actual size: 14[18] x 14[18]in
(36[46] x 36[46]cm)

Figures in square brackets refer to
larger sizes. Where only one set
of figures is given, this refers
to all sizes.

You will need

Rowan Big Wool 100% Merino wool
(approx. 87yd/80m per 100g)

1[2] x 100g balls in 84
Aurora Pink (A)

1[2] x 100g balls in 63
Lipstick Red (B)

1[2] x 100g balls in 25
Wild Berry (C)

1[2] x 100g balls in 85 Vintage (D)

9mm (UK00:US13) needles

Yarn needle for sewing up

16[20]in (40[50]cm)-long zip

16[20]in square (40[50]cm)
cushion pad

Note: Yarn amounts are based
on average requirements and
are approximate.

TO CROCHET THE ZIP

Crochet hook

4-ply yarn in colour to match zip

Fabric pen or tailor's chalk

Sharp-pointed tool

Tension

11 sts and 20 rows to 4in (10cm)
over g st.

Use larger or smaller needles if
necessary to obtain correct tension.

Abbreviations

See page 148.

Yarn note

For the larger cushion, only a
tiny bit more than one ball of yarn
in each colour is needed to complete
the stripe sequence. To save yarn
and cash, instead of completing
the stripe sequence as set, you
could simply buy one ball of yarn
in three shades and two in your
favourite colour and complete the
cushion cover with a solid triangle
in one corner.

Stripe sequence

Work 8 rows in each colour as foll:
A, B, C, D, B, A, D, C.
Repeat this stripe sequence
throughout.

Cushion cover

Using A, cast on 3 sts.
Knit 1 row.

SET INCREASE PATT

Row 1: K1, m1L, k to last st,
m1R, k1.

Row 2: Knit.

Rep rows 1 and 2 until you have 67
sts. Piece measures approx. 14[18]in
(36[46]cm) up the diagonal side.

SET STRAIGHT SECTION

Row 1: K1, m1L, k to last 3 sts,
k2tog, k1.

Row 2: Knit.

Rep rows 1 and 2 until piece
measures approx. 28[36]in (72[92]
cm) along longer side.

SET DECREASE PATT

Row 1: K1, ssk, k to last 3 sts,
k2tog, k1.

Row 2: Knit.

Rep rows 1 and 2 until 3 sts rem,
ending with row 2.
Cast off rem 3 sts.

To finish

Fold cushion in half and crochet
(see page 42) or sew zip into side
opposite the folded edge. Join
the two side seams together with
mattress stitch (see page 146).
Weave in ends and block if required.
Insert cushion pad.

CROCHETING A ZIP

1 Use a fabric pen or tailor's chalk to mark 32 points at approximately ½in (1cm) intervals along both sides of zip to match alternate stitches (between garter stitch bumps) along the cushion side, starting 1in (2.5cm) in from the closed end of the zip. Use a sharp tool to punch a small hole into each marked point.

2 Make a slip knot and insert your crochet hook into it. Push the crochet hook from back to front through the hole closest to the closed end of the zip, then insert it into the slip knot at the front of the zip, yarn over and pull it through both the slip knot and the hole.

3 Your working yarn should now be at the back of the zip while your crochet hook and working loop are on the top. Take care to work loosely, as working too tightly will cause the zip to pucker.

4 Insert the crochet hook from front to back through the next hole in the zip, yarn over and pull the yarn through the hole and through the current stitch on the hook. Repeat this step until you have worked in all the holes on one side of the zip and have a crochet chain running up the zip beside its teeth. Then repeat steps 2–4 on the other side.

5 Now, with the RS of the cushion cover facing, lay the zip in place. The crochet chain up the zip should match the stitches along one side of the cushion cover. Insert the crochet hook into the first stitch of the cushion cover and the first stitch of the zip. Yarn over and pull through the chain on the zip and the stitch of the cushion cover (1 st on hook).

6 Insert the hook into the next stitch on the cushion cover and the next chain on the zip, yarn over and pull through both of those loops (2 sts on hook), then yarn over and pull through both rem sts on hook. Repeat this step along both sides of the zip until you have crocheted it all in, then fasten off.

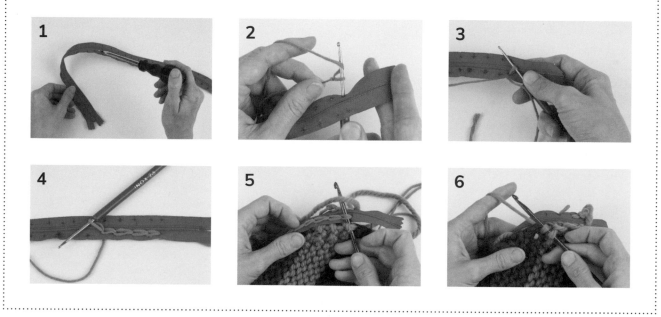

A knitting night in

Plan your perfect evening home alone with your yarn and needles.

TEA TIME
Herbal teas are a great way to relax. I love a hot peppermint tea while I'm knitting, but there are plenty of other flavours out there with different soothing and healing properties.

VIEWING PLATFORM
A quiet night in is a great time to cosy up on the sofa with a good film or a DVD box set. Plan what you're going to watch in advance so that you have more time to enjoy it while you knit.

LISTEN IN
If you prefer to keep your eyes on your knitting, why not explore the world of knitting (and non-craft) podcasts? All sorts of broadcasts and audiobooks are available online, so settle in, knit and listen to whatever you choose.

GET SOME SLEEP
If your knitting starts to frustrate you, put it down and turn your mind to something else for a while, or just go to bed and get some rest – you'll find it looks much better in the morning.

Do you ever feel like the world is full of fast, disposable fashion and constant image changes that leave you wondering who you really are? Knitting is a great way to take time to explore yourself – craft clothes to fit your shape, your size, your hopes and your dreams.

Explore

Just be me

JOMO is all about being who you are and not what other people say you should be – and this jumper is designed to celebrate just being you. The body is knitted in one piece from the bottom up, with flattering side panels and a slightly longer back hem. This is the sweater you'll cuddle up in when everything is going wrong – and wear with pride when everything's going right.

Size
To fit bust:
    34–36[38–40:42–44:46–48]in
    (86–91[97–102:107–112:117–
    122]cm)
Actual bust: 46½[51¼:56:60¼]in
    (118[130:142:153]cm)
Front length underarm to hem:
    15¾in (40cm)
Back length underarm to hem:
    18½in (47cm)
Sleeve length: 20in (51cm)
Figures in square brackets refer
to larger sizes. Where only one set
of figures is given, this applies to
all sizes.

You will need
Wool and the Gang Crazy Sexy
    Wool 100% wool (approx.
    87yd/80m per 200g)
6[7:8:8] x 200g balls in
    Mustard Sally
12mm (UK–:US17) circular needle
    40in (100cm) long
12mm (UK–:US17) double-pointed
    needles or circular needle for
    magic loop method
Stitch holders or scrap yarn
5 stitch markers
Note: Yarn amounts are based
on average requirements and
are approximate.

Tension
Approx. 6.5 sts and 11 rows to
4in (10cm) over st st. Use larger
or smaller needles if necessary
to obtain the correct tension.

Abbreviations
See page 148.

Pattern note
This jumper is knitted in the round
from the bottom up. The body is
worked first to the armholes, then
the sleeves, then they are joined to
work the yoke in one piece. Finally,
the underarms are grafted using
Kitchener stitch (see page 138).

Body

Cast on 80[88:96:104] sts. Join in the round, taking care not to twist stitches, then pm to mark start of round at centre back.

SET RIB

Set-up round: (K1, p1) 10[11:12:13] times, pm, (k1, p1) 4 times, k2, (p1, k1) 10[12:14:16] times, p1, k2, (p1, k1) 4 times, pm, (p1, k1) to last st, p1 (20[22:24:26] sts for Left back, 41[45:49:53] sts for Front, 19[21:23:25] sts for Right back). This round sets rib patt. Cont in rib as set for 5 more rounds.

SHAPE BACK HEM

In this section the Back hem is shaped using shadow-wrap short rows (see page 140), working back and forth over back section only.

Short row 1: K16[18:20:22], w&t.
Short row 2: P32[36:40:44] (across centre back start-of-round marker), w&t.
Short row 3: K to wrapped st, k wrap tog with wrapped st, w&t.

Short row 4: P to wrapped st, p wrap tog with wrapped st, w&t.
Rep rows 3 and 4 once more, then knit to end of round.

SET SIDE PANELS

You will now return to working in the round. On the first round, knit wraps tog with wrapped sts as you come to them.

Round 1: K to first side marker, sm, (k1, p1) 4 times, k2, p1, k19[23:27:31], p1, k2, (p1, k1) 4 times, sm, k to end.
Round 2: K to first side marker, sm, (p1, k1) 4 times, k2, p1, k19[23:27:31], p1, k2, (k1, p1) 4 times, sm, k to end.
These two rounds set m st side panels with (k2, p1) and (p1, k2) borders.
Note: Each k2 for the border should line up with the k2 in the single rib below.
Rep rounds 1 and 2 three more times.

SET SIDE PANEL SHAPING

Round 1: K to first side marker, sm, m st 7, k2tog, k1, p1, m1L, k19[23:27:31], m1R, p1, k1, ssk, m st 7, sm, k to end.
Round 2: K to first side marker, sm, m st 7, k2, p1, k21[25:29:33], p1, k2, m st 7, sm, k to end.
Round 3: K to first side m, sm, m st 6, k2tog, k1, p1, m1L, k21[25:29:33], m1R, p1, k1, ssk, m st 6, sm, k to end.
Round 4: K to first side m, sm, m st 6, k2, p1, k23[27:31:35], p1, k2, m st 6, sm, k to end.
Round 5: K to first side m, sm, m st 5, k2tog, k1, p1, m1L, k23[27:31:35], m1R, p1, k1, ssk, m st 5, sm, k to end.
Round 6: K to first side m, sm, m st 5, k2, p1, k25[29:33:37], p1, k2, m st 5, sm, k to end.
Round 7: K to first side m, sm, m st 4, k2tog, k1, p1, m1L, k25[29:33:37], m1R, p1, k1, ssk, m st 4, sm, k to end.
Round 8: K to first side m, sm, m st 4, k2, p1, k27[31:35:39], p1, k2, m st 4, sm, k to end.

Round 9: K to first side m, sm, m st 3, k2tog, k1, p1, m1L, k27[31:35:39], m1R, p1, k1, ssk, m st 3, sm, k to end.

Round 10: K to first side m, sm, m st 3, k2, p1, k29[33:37:41], p1, k2, m st 3, sm, k to end.

Round 11: K to first side m, sm, m st 2, k2tog, k1, p1, m1L, k29[33:37:41], m1R, p1, k1, ssk, m st 2, sm, k to end.

Round 12: K to first side m, sm, m st 2, k2, p1, k31[35:39:43], p1, k2, m st 2, sm, k to end.

Round 13: K to first side m, sm, m st 1, k2tog, k1, p1, m1L, k31[35:39:43], m1R, p1, k1, ssk, m st 1, sm, k to end.

Round 14: K to first side m, sm, m st 1, k2, p1, k33[37:41:45], p1, k2, m st 1, sm, k to end.

Round 15: K to first side m, sm, k2tog, k1, p1, m1L, k33[37:41:45], p1, k1, ssk, sm, k to end.

Round 16: K to first side m, sm, k2, p1, k35[39:43:47], p1, k2, sm, k to end.

Round 17: K to first side m, sm, k2tog, p1, m1L, k35[39:43:47], m1R, p1, ssk, sm, k to end.

Round 18: K to first side m, sm, k1, p1, k37[41:45:49], p1, k1, sm, k to end.

Round 19: K to first side m, sm, p2tog, m1L, k37[41:45:49], m1R, ssp, sm, k to end.

Round 20: K to first side m, sm, p1, k39[43:47:51], p1, sm, k to end.

Round 21: Knit.

Cont straight in st st until Body measures 15¾in (40cm) or desired length to armholes.

Set aside and make Sleeves.

Sleeves (make 2)

Cast on 16[18:18:18] sts. Join in the round, taking care not to twist sts, and pm to mark beg of round.

Round 1: (K1, p1) around.

Rep round 1 five times.

Knit 2 rounds.

SET SLEEVE SHAPING

*Next round (inc): K1, m1R, k to last stitch, m1L, k1.
Knit 7[7:5:5] rounds.
Rep from * 3[3:5:6] times, then work inc round again (26[28:32:34] sts).

Cont without shaping until Sleeve measures 20in (50cm) or desired length to armhole.
Slip first 3 and last 3[4:4:4] sts of round to holder or scrap yarn.
Set aside.

YOKE

Set-up round: K17[19:21:23] (Left back), slip next 6[7:7:7] sts to a holder, pm1, k20[21:25:27] from first sleeve holder (Left sleeve), pm2, k35[37:41:45] (Front), slip next 6[7:7:7] sts to a holder, pm3, k20[21:25:27] from second sleeve holder (Right sleeve), pm4, k16[18:20:22] (Right back). (108[116:132:144] sts)
Knit 2[3:9:8] rounds.

SET RAGLAN DECREASES

*Round 1 (dec): K to 3 sts before m, ssk, k1, sm, k1, k2tog; rep from * 3 more times, k to end (dec 8).
Knit 2[2:1:1] rounds.
Rep from * 7[8:9:10] times, then work dec round 0[0:1:1] more time (44[44:44:48] sts).

SHAPE BACK NECK

Short row 1: K to m2, sm, k1, w&t.
Short row 2: P back across beg of round marker and m4 to m3, sm, p1, w&t.
*Short row 3: K to wrapped st, k wrap tog with wrapped st, w&t.
Short row 4: P to wrapped st, p wrap tog with wrapped st, w&t.
Rep from * once, then k to end of round.
Remove all markers except for beg of round marker.

SET RIB

Note: On first rib round, work wraps tog with wrapped sts as you come to them in rib patt.
Next round: (K1, p1) around.
Rep last round 5 times.
Cast off in rib.

To finish

Slip both sets of underarm sts for Right sleeve back to two needles and join using Kitchener stitch (see page 138). Rep for Left sleeve. Weave in ends. Pin to measurements, cover with damp cloths and leave to dry.

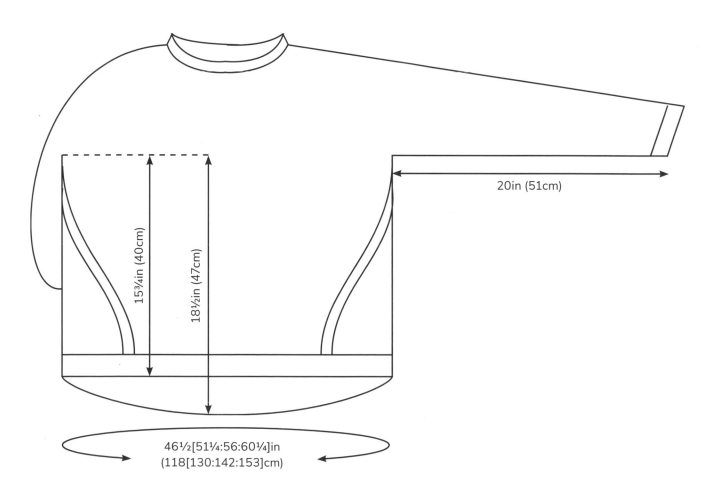

20in (51cm)

15¾in (40cm)

18½in (47cm)

46½[51¼:56:60¼]in
(118[130:142:153]cm)

Forest walk

Knitted in a beautiful dark green recycled wool that mirrors the colours of the forest, this elegant coat is perfect for keeping warm on a cold woodland walk. It also has handy pockets for collecting pretty leaves, stones and conkers.

Sizes

To fit bust:
32–34[36–38:40–44:46–48]in
(81–86[91–97:102–112:117–
122]cm)
Actual bust: 37¾[42½:47¼:52]in
(96[108:120:132]cm)
Front length: 36¼ 36¼:37:37]in
(92[92:94:94]cm)
Back length: 38½[38½:39½:39½]in
(98[98:100:100]cm)
Sleeve length: 21¾in (55cm)
(adjustable)
Figures in square brackets refer to larger sizes. Where only one figure is given, this refers to all sizes.

You will need

Wool and the Gang Heal the Wool
    100% recycled wool (approx.
    87yd/80m per 200g)
9[10:10:11] x 200g balls in
    Forest Green
12mm (UK–:US17) needles
    (I recommend a circular needle
    with a long cable as there are
    a lot of stitches, which can
    be heavy)
Spare 12mm (UK–:US17) needle
    for three-needle cast off
Stitch markers
Stitch holders
4 buttons
Note: Yarn amounts given are based on average requirements and are approximate.

Tension

7 sts and 10 rows to 4in (10cm) over st st.
Use larger or smaller needles if necessary to obtain the correct tension.

Pattern notes

This coat is worked in one piece from the bottom up. The back hem is given a flattering curve with short rows. If you prefer a straight hem, simply skip the short-row section. The skirt narrows to the waist, then the torso section is worked straight, and fronts and back divide at the armholes. Shoulder seams are joined using a three-needle cast off (see page 141). Sleeves are then picked up from the armholes, shaped using short rows and knitted down to the cuffs. Lengthen or shorten sleeves as required before making the final decreases.
Where markers are not mentioned, simply slip them.

Abbreviations

See page 148.

Pocket linings (make 2)

Cast on 10 sts.
Row 1: Knit.
Row 2: Purl.
Rep rows 1 and 2 six more times.
Slip sts to a holder or scrap yarn.

Body

Cast on 94[102:110:118] sts using the long tail method (see page 119).

SET MOSS STITCH HEM
Row 1: (K1, p1) to end.
Row 2: (P1, k1) to end.
Rep rows 1 and 2 three more times.

SHAPE BACK HEM
Set-up row (RS): (K1, p1) 3 times, k19[21:23:25], pm1, k44[48:52:56], pm2, k to last 6 sts, (k1, p1) 3 times.
Short row 1 (WS): M st 6, p to 1 st before m1 (slipping m2), w&t.
Short row 2: K to 1 st before m2, w&t.
Short row 3: P to wrapped st, p wrap tog with wrapped st, sm, w&t.
Short row 4: K to wrapped st, k wrap tog with wrapped st, sm, w&t.
Rep rows 3 and 4 once more, slipping markers as you come to them.

Next row (WS): P to last 6 sts, m st 6.

SET MAIN PATT
Note: On row 1, k wrapped st tog with wrap as you come to it.
Row 1 (RS): M st 6, k to last 6 sts, m st 6.
Row 2: M st 6, p to last 6 sts, m st 6. Rows 1 and 2 set st st patt with m st borders. Rep these 2 rows 3 more times.

SET DECREASE PATT FOR SKIRT
Dec row: *Patt as set to 3 sts before m, ssk, k1, sm, k1, k2tog; rep from * once, patt to end (dec 4).
Patt 9 rows.
Rep these 10 rows 2 more times (82[90:98:106] sts).

SET POCKETS
Next row (dec): M st 6, k2, k across 10 held sts for one pocket, slip 10 sts from Body to holder or scrap yarn, *k to 3 sts before m1, ssk, k1, sm, k1, k2tog; rep from * once, k to last 18 sts, k across 10 held sts for second pocket, slip 10 sts from Body to holder or scrap yarn, k2, m st 6.
Patt 9 rows, then work dec

row again. 74[82:90:98] sts: 20[22:24:26] for each Front and 34[38:42:46] for Back.
Next row (WS): Patt as set.
Buttonhole row (RS): M st 2, yo, patt 2 tog, m st 2, patt to end.
Next row: Patt as set, working yo from previous row in patt to form buttonhole.
Cont straight in patt for 8 rows, then rep buttonhole row.
Cont straight in patt for 7[7:5:5] more rows.

DIVIDE FOR BACK AND FRONTS
Next row (RS): M st 6, k12[14:16:18], cast off 4 sts (2 sts on each side of marker), k30[34:38:42], cast off 4 sts, k12[14:16:18], m st 6.
Turn and work on last 18[20:22:24] sts only, slipping rem sts over to scrap yarn.

LEFT FRONT
Next row (WS): M st 6, p to last 2 sts, ssp (17[19:21:23] sts).
Cont straight in patt for 8[8:10:10] rows.

SHAPE NECK

Short row 1 (RS): K to last 7 sts, w&t.
Short row 2: P to end.
Short row 3: K to 1 st before wrapped st, w&t.
Short row 4: P to end.
Short row 5: K to 1 st before last wrapped st, w&t.
Short row 6: P to end.
Next row (RS): Patt to end, working wraps tog with wrapped sts as you come to them.
Next row (WS): Cast off 10[11:12:13] sts at neck edge in patt, p to end, slip rem 7[8:9:10] sts to holder or scrap yarn.

RIGHT FRONT

Slip held sts for Right front back to holder and rejoin yarn with RS facing.
Next row (RS dec): M st 6, k to last 2 sts, k2tog (17[19:21:23] sts).
Cont straight in patt for 8[8:10:10] rows, working buttonhole in border of 1st[1st:5th:5th] of these rows as folls: Patt to last 6 sts, m st 3, yo, patt2tog, patt 1.

SHAPE NECK

Short row 1 (WS): P to last 7 sts, w&t.
Short row 2: K to end.
Short row 3: P to 1 st before wrapped st, w&t.
Short row 4: K to end.
Short row 5: P to 1 st before last wrapped st, w&t.
Short row 6: K to end.
Next row (WS): Patt to end, working wraps tog with wrapped sts as you come to them.
Next row (RS): Cast off 10[11:12:13] sts in patt for neck, k to end, slip rem 7[8:9:10] sts to a holder.

BACK

Slip Back sts to needles and rejoin yarn with RS facing.
Next row (RS dec): Ssk, k to last 2 sts, k2tog (28[32:36:40] sts).
Work straight for 11[11:13:13] rows.

SHAPE NECK

Short row 1 (RS): K10[12:14:16], w&t.
Short row 2: P to end.
Short row 3: K to 2 sts before wrapped st, w&t.
Short row 4: P to end.

JOIN SHOULDER SEAMS

Slip held sts for Left back and Left front shoulders back to needles and join using three-needle cast-off (see page 141).

Repeat for Right back and Right front shoulder sts.

Sleeves (both alike)

Starting at underarm, pick up and knit 22[22:24:24] sts around armhole, pm1 to mark beg of round and pm2 after 11[11:12:12] sts to mark top of shoulder.

Knit 1 round.

SHAPE SLEEVE CAP

Short row 1: K to 3 sts after m2, w&t.

Short row 2: P to 3 sts after m2, w&t.

Short row 3: K to wrapped st, k wrap tog with wrapped st, w&t.

Short row 4: P to wrapped st, p wrap tog with wrapped st, w&t.

Rep rows 3 and 4 until you have 3 sts unworked before and after m1. Remove m2.

K to end of round, knitting together any rem wraps with wrapped sts. Cont straight in st st until Sleeve measures approx. 17[17:16¼:16¼]in (43[43:41:41]cm) or 4¾[4¾:5½:5½] in (12[12:14:14]cm) less than desired length.

SHAPE SLEEVE

Next round: K1, k2tog, k to 3 sts before m1, ssk, k1 (20[20:22:22] sts).

Next round: Knit.

Rep the last 2 rounds 1[1:2:2] more times (18 sts).

SET CUFF

Round 1: (K1, p1) around.

Round 2: (P1, k1) around.

Rep rounds 1 and 2 three more times.

Cast off loosely in patt.

Short row 5: K to end, working wraps tog with wrapped sts as you come to them.

Short row 6: P10[12:14:16], w&t.

Short row 7: K to end.

Short row 8: P to 2 sts before wrapped st, w&t.

Short row 9: K to end.

Short row 10: P across all sts, working wraps tog with wrapped sts as you come to them.

Next row (RS): K7[8:9:10], slip sts just worked to a holder, cast off next 14[16:18:20] sts, k to end, slip rem 7[8:9:10] sts to a holder.

To finish

Weave in ends. Sew buttons on button band to match buttonholes.

POCKET EDGING (BOTH ALIKE)
Slip pocket sts from holder back to needle.

Row 1: (K1, p1) to end.
Row 2: (P1, k1) to end.
Rep rows 1 and 2 once more.
Cast off loosely in patt.
Sew sides of edging neatly to RS of cardigan. Sew pocket lining to WS. Weave in rem ends and block to measurements.

Neckband

With RS facing, starting at Right front neck edge, pick up and knit 6 sts across buttonhole band, 6 sts to shoulder seam, 16[16:18:18] sts across Back neck, 6 sts across Left front neck and 6 sts across button band (40[40:42:42] sts).

Row 1 (WS): (K1, p1) to end.
Row 2: (P1, k1) to end.
Row 3 (buttonhole): (K1, p1) to last 4 sts, k2tog, yo, k1, p1.
Row 4: As row 2, working yo from previous row in patt to form buttonhole.
Rep rows 1 and 2 once more.
Next row (WS dec): P2tog, (k1, p1) to last 2 sts, k2tog (38[38:40:40] sts).
Cast off loosely in patt.

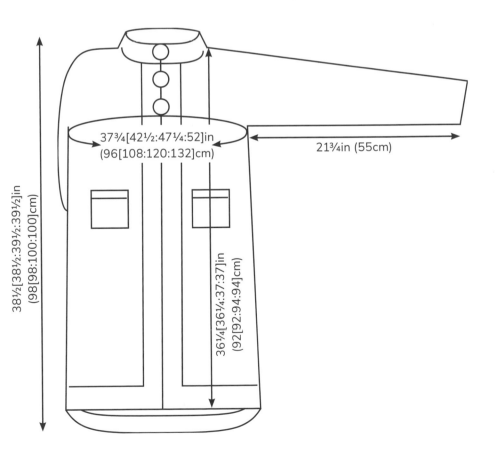

37¾[42½:47¼:52]in
(96[108:120:132]cm)

21¾in (55cm)

38½[38½:39½:39½]in (98[98:100:100]cm)

36¼[36¼:37:37]in (92[92:94:94]cm)

Me-time

Sometimes it can be hard to grab a few moments of me-time – and if you want that lovely feeling of accomplishment from your precious minutes alone, these pretty and quick-to-knit lace mitts could be just the ticket.

Size
To fit: Average adult
Circumference: 7in (18cm)
Length: 8¾in (22cm)

You will need
Rowan Big Wool 100% Merino wool
    (approx. 87yd/80m per 100g)
1 x 100g ball in 078 Yoke
8mm (UK0:US11) and 9mm
    (UK00:US13) double-pointed or
    circular needles
Stitch holder
Stitch markers
Note: Yarn amounts given are based
on average requirements and are
approximate.

Tension
11 sts and 7 rows to 4in (10cm) over
pattern using 9mm (UK00:US13)
needles. Use larger or smaller
needles if necessary to obtain
the correct tension.

Abbreviations
See page 148.

Left mitten

Using 8mm (UK0:US11) needles, cast on 20 sts. Join to work in the round, taking care not to twist sts, and pm to mark beg of round.

Rib round: (P2, k2) around.
Rep rib round 1 more time.
Change to 9mm (UK00:US13) needles.

SET MAIN PATTERN

Round 1: P2, k2, yo, skpo, k2, (p2, k2) 3 times.
Rounds 2 and 4: P2, k6, (p2, k2) 3 times.
Round 3: P2, k2, k2tog, yo, k2, (p2, k2) 3 times.
These 4 rounds form patt.
Rep these 4 rounds once more, then cont in patt as set while shaping gusset and thumbhole.**

SHAPE GUSSET

Next round: Pfb, p1, patt to end (21 sts).
Next round: P3, k6, (p2, k2) 3 times.
Next round (round 3 of patt): Pfb, p2, patt to end (22 sts).
Next round: P4, k6, (p2, k2) 3 times.

Cont straight in patt for 2 more 4-round patt reps, working p4 at start of each round instead of p2.

SHAPE THUMBHOLE

Next round: Sl4 sts to a holder, cast on 2 sts, patt to end (20 sts).

***HAND

Work rest of this patt rep and one more patt rep.
Change to 8mm (UK0:US11) needles.
Work rib round twice.
Cast off in rib.

LEFT THUMB

Using 8mm (UK0:US11) needles, slip 4 sts from holder to needle, pick up and knit 1 st from side of thumbhole, 2 across cast-on sts and 1 st from other side of thumbhole (8 sts).
Pm to mark beg of round.****
Rib round: (K2, p2) around.
Rep this round 3 times.
Cast off loosely in rib.

Right mitten

Work as for Left mitten to **.

SHAPE GUSSET

Next round: P2, k2, yo, skpo, k2,

p1, pfb, pm, patt to end (21 sts).
Next round: P2, k6, p3, sm, k2, (p2, k2) twice.
Next round (round 3 of patt): P2, k2, k2tog, yo, k2, p2, pfb, sm k2, (p2, k2) twice (22 sts).
Next round: P2, k6, p4, sm, k2, (p2, k2) twice.
Cont straight in patt for two more 4-round patt reps, working p4 instead of p2 as set by last round.

SHAPE THUMBHOLE

Next round: Patt to 4 sts before m, sl4 sts to a holder, cast on 2 sts, patt to end (20 sts).
Work as for Left mitten from ***
to end.

RIGHT THUMB

Work as Left thumb to ****.
Rib round: (P2, k2) around.
Rep this round 3 times.
Cast off loosely in rib.

To finish

Weave in ends.

5 inspiring knitters

There are so many inspiring designers and knitters out there that it feels almost mean-spirited to just pick five, but think of these as just a taster.

1

DEBBIE STOLLER

Debbie Stoller is the co-founder of feminist magazine *Bust* and author of the *Stitch 'n Bitch* series of knitting books. Without her vision of a new, fresh, young and fun style of knitting, I would never have got caught up in the craft that has helped make me the person I am today.

2

ERIKA KNIGHT

From designing for pop royalty in the 1980s to standing up for homegrown British wool today, Erika is a moral inspiration as well as a fashion icon. Her simple, stylish designs are enduring classics that you can knit again and again.

3

ELIZABETH ZIMMERMANN

Knitting Without Tears is a must-read for anyone who struggles with following patterns or just wants to write their own. It is packed with the sort of helpful advice everyone needs, such as: 'Take out the needle; without screaming, please.'

4

KRISTA SUH

The young woman behind the campaigning Pussyhat Project – which turned streets around the world into seas of bright pink as women marched for their rights – has also written a funny, personal and motivating book encouraging women and girls to stand up to their own inner critics and believe in themselves: *DIY Rules for a WTF World*.

5

MARGARET WHITE

No one else in the knitting world will have heard of my granny, Margaret. But she taught me to knit, brightened my childhood with adorable personalized knits, bought me my first stitch dictionary and was my knitting guru in the dark days before YouTube. Probably the most inspiring knitter in the world is the person who personally taught you how to knit.

Cherish

This cowl is perfect for wrapping up in when you need a bit of extra comfort. Easy to knit in the round, with a pretty moss stitch texture, it is a big loop designed to be wrapped around the neck twice for extra warmth and style.

Size
Circumference: 68in (172cm)
Depth: 8¾in (22cm)

You will need
Loopy Mango Merino No 5 100%
    Merino wool (approx. 74yd/68m
    per 150g)
1 x 150g ball in Dorian Gray (A)
1 x 150g ball in Mrs Orange (B)
15mm (UK–:US19) circular needle
    at least 30in (80cm) long
Stitch marker
Note: Yarn amounts given are based
on average requirements and are
approximate.

Tension
5 sts and 11 rounds to 4in (10cm).
Use larger or smaller needles
if necessary to obtain the
correct tension.

Abbreviations
See page 148.

Cowl
Using A, cast on 90 sts. Join in the round, taking care not to twist sts, and pm to mark beg of round.
Knit 1 round.

SET MOSS STITCH PATTERN
Rounds 1 and 2: (K1, p1) around.
Rounds 3 and 4: (P1, k1) around.
Rep rounds 1–4 once, then rounds 1 and 2 again.
Knit 2 rounds.
Cut A and join B.
Knit 2 rounds.

SET MOSS STITCH PATTERN
Rep rounds 1–4 twice, then rounds 1 and 2 again.
Knit 1 round.
Cast off.

To finish
Weave in ends neatly.
Block if required.

Craft yourself well

MORE AND MORE PEOPLE are taking up knitting for the sense of wellbeing it gives them. They use it as part of their daily mindfulness practice and as a way to express themselves creatively in lives that can be far too busy and packed with mundane chores.

Mindfulness is defined as a mental state achieved by focusing one's awareness on the present moment, while calmly acknowledging and accepting one's feelings, thoughts and bodily sensations. It is widely used as a therapeutic technique both by medical professionals and countless ordinary people in their daily lives. It can boost mental wellbeing by helping us to reconnect with our bodies, see things around us that have been taken for granted afresh and come to understand ourselves better. Mindfulness can help us to stand back from our own thought patterns so we can see them more clearly, picking out those that are unhelpful and beginning to work through them.

The beneficial effects of knitting are just as well documented as those of mindfulness. Medical studies and popular polls alike attest to the soothing nature of its rhythmic movements, the comfort of soft yarn passing through your fingers and the sense of achievement that comes from a completed project.

Knitting can help to ground us in the present moment, which is the essence of mindfulness. Choosing designs – or making our own – is creative, and there is joy to be found in browsing different textures and colours as we pick the perfect yarn for our next project. As we work we see the knitting gradually growing, feel the texture of yarn and needles as they meet, hear the soft click-clack of metal, wooden or plastic needles, and – my favourite – smell the wonderful smells of the yarn we're working with, whether it's the slightly tangy edge of bold acid-dyed fibres, the farmy tones of undyed wool straight from the sheep or the soft, clean notes of a neat, plain ball of yarn.

Staying in touch with our senses as we knit gives us a break from all the things that assail us day in, day out. If you need time out from the pinging of emails, text messages and social media alerts, the hard shininess of computers, mobile phones, cars and trains, or the super-fast pace of modern life, knitting can be your holiday.

"Almost everything will work again if you unplug it for a few minutes – including you."

ANNE LAMOTT

FIVE-MINUTE MINDFUL KNIT

Find five minutes in your busy day to try this simple exercise in mindful knitting.

1 Find a quiet space where you can sit comfortably, ideally without interruptions, and get comfortable with your knitting in your lap.

2 Before you start, sit with your hands resting on your yarn, close your eyes and take a deep breath into the pit of your stomach, then release it slowly or sigh it out. Repeat this a few times, feeling yourself settling into the time and place where you are right now.

3 Now pick up your knitting. Still thinking about breathing slowly and deeply, knit a few stitches as you take your next in-breath, then stop and rest as you breathe out.

4 As you repeat step three, become aware of the physical sensations you are experiencing as you knit, and of any thoughts that are coming into your mind. As each thought comes to you, acknowledge it calmly but do not take it any further. Let it go and return your attention to your knitting.

5 End your practice by once again taking a few deep breaths, then sit for a few moments with your eyes open before returning to your regular routine.

Feel the rhythm

Brioche is a technique that is often regarded as tricky; it is actually quite straightforward, but looks impressive. Once you get into the rhythm – as you're sure to while making this super-soft winter warmer – it can be soothing and meditative. Giant scarves like the one pictured (made in the larger size) are all the rage; for more standard-length neckwear, try the smaller size.

Size
Width: 12in (30cm)
Length: 80[122]in (204[310]cm)
Figures in square brackets refer to larger size. Where only one figure is given, this refers to both sizes.

You will need
Cascade Spuntaneous 100% wool
    (approx. 109yd/100m per 200g)
2[3] x 200g hanks in 17 Cactus
    Flower (A)
2[3] x 200g hanks in 16 Acai (B)
10mm (UK000:US15) circular needle
Note: Yarn amounts given are based on average requirements and are approximate.

Tension
8 sts and 18 rows to 4in (10cm) over brioche rib.
Tension is not critical to this project.

Pattern note
Refer to page 133 for more instructions on brioche knitting.

Abbreviations
brk1 = brioche knit 1: knit slipped st from previous row tog with yarn over.
brp1 = brioche purl 1: purl slipped st from previous row tog with yarn over.
sl1yo = bring yarn to front of work, slip next st pwise: if the next st is a knit st, take the yarn over the top of the needle to work the next st; if it is a purl st, take the yarn away from you over the needle and bring it back to the front in between the two needles ready to work the next st. For standard abbreviations, see page 148.

Pattern note
The scarf is completely reversible, but for the purposes of this pattern it has a RS and a WS marked. You may wish to place a stitch marker on the RS to help you keep track of your work during the two-colour section.

Scarf

Cast on 24 sts in A.

Set-up row: K1, (sl1yo, k1) to last st, k1.

SET ONE-COLOUR SECTION

Row 1: K1, (sl1yo, brk1) to last st, k1.

Rep row 1 until you have used 1[2] skeins of A.

SET TWO-COLOUR SECTION

Row 1 (RS): Using A, work as row 1 above, then slide sts back to other end of needle ready to work RS row again.

Row 2 (RS): Using B, k1, (brp1, sl1yo) to last st, k1, turn.

Row 3 (WS): Using A, k1, (brp1, sl1yo) to last st, k1, slide sts back to other end of needle ready to work WS row again.

Row 4 (WS): Using B, k1, (sl1yo, brk1) to last st, k1.

Rep rows 1–4 until you have used 1 skein each of A and B in this section (2[3] skeins of A in total), then cont in B only.

Work one-colour section again but in B until you have used nearly all your yarn.

Cast off as folls: K1, *p1, pass first st on RH needle over second, brk1, pass first st on RH needle over second; rep from * to last st, k1, pass first st over second, fasten off.

To finish

Weave in ends neatly in the correct colour sections.

Switch off

This sweetly simple fishtail lace pattern and beautiful kettle-dyed yarn combine to create a striking slouchy beanie. Perfect for keeping cosy while exploring.

Size
To fit: Average adult
Circumference: 14¼in (36cm)
  (stretchy)
Depth: 9in (23cm)

You will need
Malabrigo Mecha 100% Merino
  superwash wool (approx.
  131yd/120m per 100g)
1 x 100g hank in 412 Teal Feather
7mm (UK2:US10½) double-pointed
  or circular needles
Stitch marker
Note: Yarn amounts given are based
on average requirements and are
approximate.

Tension
16 sts and 25 rows to 4in (10cm)
over pattern.
Use larger or smaller needles
if necessary to obtain the
correct tension.

Abbreviations
See page 148.

Hat
Cast on 60 sts. Join to work in
the round, taking care not to
twist stitches, and pm to mark
start of round.
Rib round: (K1, p1) around.
Rep rib round until piece measures
approx. 2½in (6.5cm).
Knit 1 round.

SET FISHTAIL STITCH PATTERN
Round 1: (Yo, k3, sk2po, k3, yo, k1)
6 times around.
Round 2 and every alt round: Knit.
Round 3: (K1, yo, k2, sk2po, k2, yo,
k2) 6 times around.
Round 5: (K2, yo, k1, sk2po, k1, yo,
k3) 6 times around.
Round 7: (K3, yo, sk2po, yo, k4) 6
times around.
These 8 rounds form patt. Rep these
8 rounds 3 more times.

SHAPE CROWN
Round 1: (K8, k2tog) around
(54 sts).
Round 2: (K7, k2tog) around
(48 sts).
Round 3: (K6, k2tog) around
(42 sts).
Round 4: (K5, k2tog) around
(36 sts).
Round 5: (K4, k2tog) around
(30 sts).
Round 6: (K3, k2tog) around
(24 sts).
Round 7: (K2, k2tog) around
(18 sts).
Round 8: (K1, k2tog) around
(12 sts).
Round 9: (K2tog) around (6 sts).
Break yarn, thread through rem
6 sts and pull tight to fasten off.

To finish
Weave in ends neatly. Block
to open out lace pattern.

I knit anywhere

My house is full of project bags. The best are of a size and sturdiness that means I can grab them as I'm running out of the house to make sure I am never without something to knit. Who knows when you might get caught in a train strike, a traffic jam or a dentist's waiting room and need something to occupy your time? Knitted bags aren't always the most resilient, but this one combines a strong recycled wool with a sturdy slip stitch pattern, so will stand up to a bit of rough treatment. It is big enough for small to medium projects such as socks, shawls or lightweight jumpers. The handle is also wide enough to slip over your wrist for bus stop or train platform knitting.

Size
Width: 9in (23cm)
Depth: 10½in (27cm)

You will need
Wool and the Gang Lil' Heal the
    Wool 100% recycled wool
    (approx. 87yd/80m per 100g)
1 x 100g ball in Curasao Blue (A)
1 x 100g ball in Charcoal (B)
6.5mm (UK3:US10½) double-
    pointed or circular needles
Stitch marker
Note: Yarn amounts given are based
on average requirements and are
approximate.

Tension
13 sts and 24 rows to 4in (10cm)
over pattern. Use larger or smaller
needles if necessary to obtain the
correct tension.

Abbreviations
See page 148.

Bag
Using A, cast on 60 sts using Judy's magic cast-on (see page 121). Pm to mark beg of round.
Knit 1 round, knitting any sts with back loops ahead of front loops tbl.

SET SLIP STITCH PATTERN
Rounds 1, 2, 5 and 6: Knit in A.
Round 3: Using B, (k3, sl1p wyib) around.
Round 4: Using B, (p3, sl1p wyib) around.
Round 7: Using B, (k1, sl1p wyib, k2) around.
Round 8: Using B, (p1, sl1p wyib, p2) around.
These 8 rounds form patt. Rep these 8 rounds 5 more times, then work rounds 1 and 2 once more. Piece measures approx. 8¼in (21cm). Break B and cont in A only.

SET HANDLES
*Next round: Ssk, k8, cast off 10 sts (1 st left on RH needle), k7, k2tog. 30 sts rem unworked. Turn and work on sts just worked only.
Next row: K9, cast on 10 sts, k to end (28 sts).
Next row: Knit.
Next row: Ssk, k to last 2 sts, k2tog (26 sts).
Next row: Knit.
Rep last 2 rows 3 more times (20 sts).
Cast off.
Rejoin yarn to rem 30 sts with the RS facing and rep from * to work second handle to match first.

To finish
Weave in ends neatly. Block if required.

MAKE YOUR OWN STITCH MARKERS

I love working with chunky yarn on larger needles, but when I came to work on this book and needed lots of stitch markers, I struggled to find ones that would fit my knitting. So I decided to make my own. There's a very cheap and cheerful way of doing this, which is simply to make a loop of yarn and knot it – but it's not particularly attractive or hardwearing, so I made mine a little prettier.

Making beaded stitch markers is simple, enjoyable and much quicker than knitting, so it makes for a fun break. You could even add letters or numbers to help you keep your markers in order. If you live near a good jewellery-making shop you'll find everything you need there. Otherwise, you can get all the supplies online.

You will need
Split rings in the diameter you need
  (I used 12mm and 20mm)
Ball-head pins
Beads
Round-nose pliers

1 Thread beads onto your ball-head pin, leaving at least 1in (2.5cm) free.

2 Pinch the end of the ball-head pin between the plier tips then wind it around the tip until you have created a firm yet narrow loop.

3 Slide this on to your split ring.

4 Now you have beautiful stitch markers that are quick to make and look lovely!

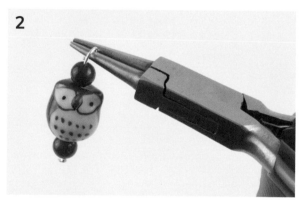

Places you can knit

Once you have got to grips with knitting, you may want to do it all the time. Here are a few places I've enjoyed knitting that you might like to try:

- On the train or bus

- In waiting rooms

- In the car (if you're the passenger)

- At the beach

- In the park

- In and outside cafés and pubs

- In the library (if you can knit without looking at your work, you could even read at the same time)

- At the zoo

- But best of all, at home on the sofa!

"Joy comes to us in moments – ordinary moments. We risk missing out on joy when we get too busy chasing down the extraordinary."

BRENÉ BROWN

Making things for others doubles
the pleasure: your joy in making
is matched by their joy in wearing.
This selection of gifts is designed
to wrap your favourite people up
in your love, wherever they may be.

Share

Hearts and diamonds

Family life can certainly be a bit of a rollercoaster ride sometimes, but there's nothing we want more for our loved ones than for them to feel part of the family and surrounded by love – so wrap them up in these cosy and snuggly sweaters and shower them with beautiful hearts and diamonds.

Sizes

To fit age: 2–4[5–7:8–12:Adult size S:M:L:XL:XXL:2XL]

To fit chest: 21½–24[24½–27:27½–31:32–34:36–38:40–42:44–46:48–50:52–54]in (55–61[62–69:70–79:81–86:91–97:102–107:112–117:122–127:132–137]cm)

Actual chest: 26[29¼:33:37:41:44½:48:52:55½]in (66[74:84:94:104:113:122:132:141]cm)

Length: 13¼[15¾:20:24:24:25¼:26½:27¼:27½]in (34[40:51:61:61:64:67:69:70]cm)

Sleeve length: 12[15:17¾:19¾:19¾:19¾:19¾:20½:20½]in (30[38:45:50:50:50:50:52:52]cm)

Figures in square brackets refer to larger sizes. Where only one set of figures is given, this refers to all sizes.

You will need

Rico Essentials Super Super Chunky 50% acrylic, 50% wool (approx. 109yd/100m per 100g)

2[3:3:4:5:5:6:6:7] x 100g balls in A

1 x 100g ball in B

1 x 100g ball in C

8mm (UK0:US11) and 10mm (UK000:US15) circular needles at least 40in (100cm) long

Stitch markers

Stitch holders

Scrap yarn

Note: Yarn amounts given are based on average requirements and are approximate.

Tension

8.5 sts and 10 rows to 4in (10cm) over st st/Fairisle patt using 10mm (UK000:US15) needles.

8.5 sts and 10 rows to 4in (10cm) over two-colour brioche patt using 8mm (UK0:US11) needles. Use larger or smaller needles if necessary to obtain the correct tension.

Pattern note

Refer to page 133 for more instructions on brioche knitting.

Abbreviations

brk1 = brioche knit 1: knit the slipped stitch and yo from the previous round together.

brp1 = brioche purl 1: purl the slipped stitch and yo from the previous round together.

sl1yo = bring yarn to front of work, slip next st pwise: if the next st is a knit st, take the yarn over the top of the needle to work the next st; if it is a purl st, take the yarn away from you over the needle and bring it back to the front in between the two needles ready to work the next st. For standard abbreviations, see page 148.

Pattern note

This pattern can be knitted in a range of shades: Yarn A is the main colour; B is the colour for the Fairisle design, and C is the contrast shade in the brioche ribbing and elsewhere. The samples here are shown in sizes 2 and 5. In size 2, A = 01 Cream, B = 022 Lilac and C = 11 Dark Pink. In size 5, A – 027 Silver Grey, B = 07 Dark Grey and C = 11 Dark Pink.

Two-colour brioche rib

Worked in the round:

Set-up round 1: Using A (k1, sl1yo) around.

Set-up round 2: Join C at the back, then bring to the front between sts and work as foll: (sl1yo, brp1) around.

Round 3: With A (brk1, sl1yo) around.

Round 4: With C (sl1yo, brp1) around.

Rounds 3 and 4 form patt and are repeated.

Body

Using 8mm (UK0:US11) needles and A, cast on 56[64:72:80:88:96:104:112:120] sts. Join to work in the round, taking care not to twist sts, and pm to mark beg of round.

SET TWO-COLOUR BRIOCHE

Work 2 set-up rounds once, then work rounds 3 and 4 of Two-colour brioche rib patt 3[3:3:5:5:5:5:5:5] times across all sts.

Change to 10mm (UK000:US15) needles.

Next round: Using A, (brk1, k1) around.

SET HEARTS AND DIAMONDS PATT

Using A and B, work 3 rounds of Hearts and Diamonds patt from Chart 7[8:9:10:11:12:13:14:15] times around.

Using A, knit straight until piece measures 8[9½:12:15:15:15:15¾:15¾:15¾]in (20[24:30:38:38:38:40:40:40]cm) or desired length to underarm.

Set aside and work Sleeves.

Sleeves (make 2)

Using 8mm (UK0:US11) needles and A, cast on 10[12:14:16:16:18:18:20:20] sts. Join to work in the round, taking care not to twist sts, and pm for beg of round.

Work Two-colour brioche patt as set for Body.

Change to 10mm (UK000:US15) needles.

SIZES 1–3 ONLY

Next round (inc): Using A, brk1, m1L, (k1, brk1) to last st, m1R, k1. (12[14:16] sts)

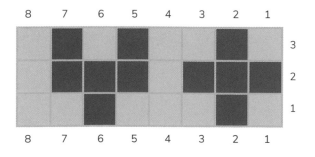

8	7	6	5	4	3	2	1	
	B		B			B		3
	B	B			B	B	B	2
		B				B		1
8	7	6	5	4	3	2	1	

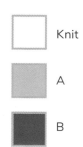

☐	Knit
▨	A
■	B

TIP

Catch the yarn not in use with the working yarn every 2 or 3 sts to avoid long floats at the back of the work and to keep the tension correct.

TIP

To work out decreases, take the number of stitches you currently have and divide that by the number of stitches you need to decrease,
eg: 88 ÷ 28 = 3.14

Round this down to the nearest whole number – in this case 3.

Now multiply 28 by 3 = 84.

Subtract this number from your original stitch count 88 – 84 = 4.

This means that you will work your 28 decreases over 84 sts and have 4 left over. You may want to work those 4 sts all in one go at the start or end of the round, or split them so that you work 2 at each end. The remaining 84 sts now need to decrease one in every three stitches – so work (k1, k2tog) across those 84 sts.

Alternatively, you could let the internet take the strain; visit one of the many websites that will work it out for you, such as worldknits.com.

SIZES 4–9 ONLY
Next round: Using A, (brk1, k1) around.
ALL SIZES
12[14:16:16:16:18:18:20:20] sts.
HEARTS AND DIAMONDS PATT
Next round: K2[1:0:0:0:1:1:2:2], work Hearts and Diamonds patt starting on st 1[5:1:1:1:1:1:1:1], k2[1:0:0:0:1:1:2:2].
Work 2 more rounds of Hearts and Diamonds patt as set.
Knit 1 round in A only.
Next round (inc): Using A, k1, m1L, k to last st, m1R, k1. Knit 3 rounds.
Rep last 3 rounds 1[2:2:3:5:5:6:6:8] times, then work inc round again (18[22:24:26:30:32:34:36:40] sts).
Cont straight in A until Sleeve measures 12[15:17¾:19¾: 19¾:19¾:19¾:20½:20½]in (30[38:45:50:50:50:50:52:52]cm) or desired length to underarm.
Slip 2[3:3:3:4:4:4:4:5] sts on each side of beg of round marker to a stitch holder, then slip rem sts to scrap yarn ready to join for yoke. 14[16:18:20:22:24:26:28:30] sts on scrap yarn.

JOIN YOKE

Using A, k12[13:15:17:18:20:
22:24:25] from Body holder (Right
back), sl4[6:6:6:8:8:8:8:10] sts
to holder for underarm, k across
14[16:18:20:22:24:26:28:30] Sleeve
sts on scrap yarn (Right sleeve),
k24[26:30:34:36:40:44:48:50] Body
sts for Front, sl4[6:6:6:8:8:8:8:10]
sts to holder for underarm, k across
14[16:18:20:22:24:26:28:30] Sleeve
sts on scrap yarn (Left sleeve),
k12[13:15:17:18:20:22:24:25] Body
sts (Left back) (76[84:96:108:116:
128:140:152:160] sts).
Work 2[4:1:3:3:6:7:9:10] rounds
straight in A.

SET YOKE PATTERN AND
SHAPING
SIZES 1 AND 2 ONLY
Next round (dec): Knit in C, dec
20[28] sts evenly around (56 sts).
SIZES 3–9 ONLY
Next round: Knit in C.

ALL SIZES
Next round: Purl in C.
Next round: Knit in A.
SIZES 3–9 ONLY
Next round: (K1A, k1B) around.
Next round: Knit in A.
Next round (dec): Knit in A,
dec 32[28:36:40:52:56:56] sts
evenly around
(64[80:80:88:88:96:104] sts).
Next round: Knit in A.
ALL SIZES
Join B and work Hearts and
Diamonds patt from Chart
7[7:8:10:10:11:11:12:13] times
around over next 3 rounds.
Next round: Knit in A.
Next round (dec): Knit in A,
dec 16[16:8:24:24:32:32:32:32]
sts evenly around
(40[40:56:56:56:56:56:64:72] sts).

SIZES 3–9 ONLY
Next round: Knit in A.
ALL SIZES
Next round: (K1A, k1B) around.
Next round: Knit in A.
SIZES 3–9 ONLY
Next round: Knit in C.
Next round: Purl in C.
Next round: Knit in A.
ALL SIZES
Next round (dec): Knit in A,
dec 16[16:16:16:16:12:12:16:24]
sts evenly around
(24[24:40:40:40:44:44:48:48] sts).
Next round: Knit in A.
Change to 8mm (UK0:US11)
needles.
Work 2 set-up rounds of Two-colour
brioche rib, then rep rounds 3 and 4
3[3:3:5:5:5:5:5:5] times.

Cast off in brioche rib as foll: brk1,
*p1, k 2 sts on RH needle tog tbl,
brk1, k 2 sts on RH needle tog tbl;
rep from * to last st, p1, k 2 sts on
RH needle tog tbl, fasten off.

To finish
Graft underarm sts using Kitchener
stitch (see page 138). Weave in
ends. Pin out to measurements,
cover with damp cloths and
leave to dry.

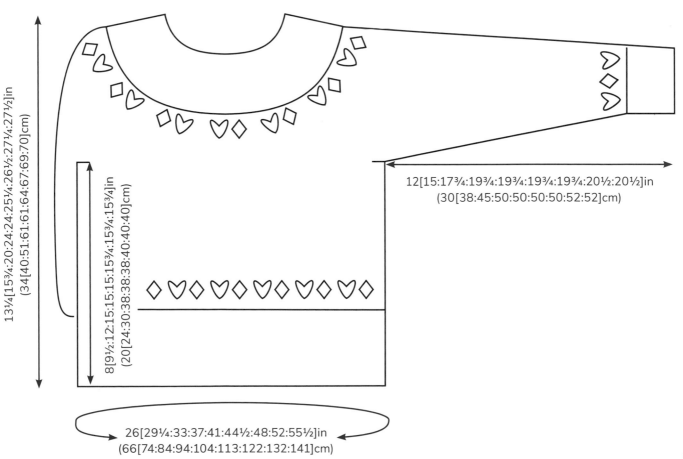

13¼[15¾:20:24:25¼:26½:27¼:27½]in
(34[40:51:61:64:67:69:70]cm)

8[9½:12:15:15:15:15¾:15¾:15¾]in
(20[24:30:38:38:38:40:40:40]cm)

12[15:17¾:19¾:19¾:19¾:19¾:20½:20½]in
(30[38:45:50:50:50:50:52:52]cm)

26[29¼:33:37:41:44½:48:52:55½]in
(66[74:84:94:104:113:122:132:141]cm)

85

"The most precious gift you can give someone is the gift of your time and attention."

NICKY GUMBEL

Knit for a cause

One of the many wonderful things about knitting is that it's something you can do all on your own. I first got into knitting as a teenager, and while I was doing it to create items that fitted in with the grunge trend of the early 1990s but are best glossed over now, it was also a great thing for an only child with busy parents to do alone in her room with an audio book.

As an adult, I returned to the craft at a time when I had moved abroad for work, leaving behind friends, family and a fairly new boyfriend who is now my husband and the father of my children. After years of increasingly unsatisfactory flat shares, I was delighted to have finally rented an apartment of my own and relished the privacy and the space. But I also found myself alone an awful lot.

It wasn't long before some balls of soft, dusky pink yarn caught my eye, sitting in appealing baskets outside a little wool shop near my home in Vienna's arty and bohemian seventh district. The friendly owner quickly set me up with matching circular needles, and I was away.

It wasn't just the comfort of the yarn running through my hands, or the rhythmic movements that calmed me on nights when I couldn't relax after a stressful day in my job at an international newswire. Knitting made me feel close to the family and friends I'd left behind. That dusky pink yarn became a scarf for my best friend, and each time I'd work on it I'd think of her. I went on to knit a misjudged stocking stitch scarf for my boyfriend (which he dutifully wore), followed by a chunky sweater. He also wore this

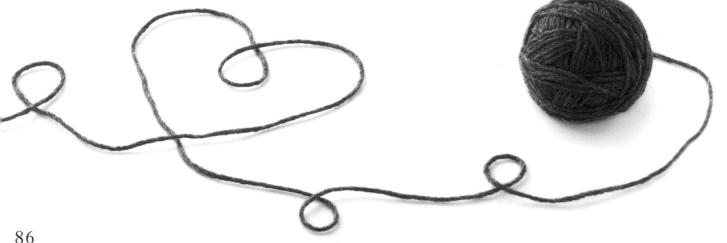

once or twice, even though I got the neckline wrong and it looked like an Elizabethan ruff – this is undoubtedly part of the reason why we are now happily married.

I still like knitting for other people. I like to feel that every stitch is infused with a little bit of love, so that when that special someone's head, hands, neck or body are warmed by the garment their heart will be warmed by the friendship behind it. Sure, it's fun to knit for myself and think how much I'll enjoy wearing that garment – especially if one of the big knitting shows is coming up, where everyone shows up in their wonderful creations – but it's just not the same as the sense of connection I get from knitting for the people I love.

Lately, however, I've been feeling that I need to expand my list of knitting recipients. After all, hand-knitted gifts are not disposable and my friends have only one head, neck and set of hands and feet each – not to mention limited wardrobe space. But there are plenty of people out there who do need more woolly goodness in their lives, and my next project is to turn my skills their way.

The internet is packed with inspiring stories of knitters crafting for others, and you are sure to find someone who can use your knitterly help. Some big-hearted knitters knit for babies – premature, stillborn and even perfectly ordinary ones who just need a little extra help. They knit toys and clothes for children who have lost their homes due to war or famine. They make warm outerwear for rough sleepers and even craft waterproof mats for them from old plastic bags – helping out and helping the environment at the same time. They knit socks for cancer patients and soft hats for those who have lost their hair when undergoing chemotherapy. They knit blankets and accessories for elderly people struggling to keep warm, and make muffs that comfort people suffering with dementia. There is simply no end to the goodness that knitting can spread.

HOW CAN I HELP?

If you'd like to knit for a good cause but aren't sure how to get started, try these steps:

- Contact your local hospital and ask if any patients might need your knits. Be sure to ask if the hospital has special guidelines for knits, as there can be strict safety rules, especially when it comes to knitting for babies or people with dementia.

- Get in touch with local community organizations. Charities, churches and other places of worship will have close links with the communities they serve and will know where help is needed.

- Try your local yarn shop. They are bound to have heard of, or be involved with, any local drives for knitted goods.

Wrap it up

Wrap up warm in this beautifully cosy cabled cardigan, knitted with two strands of exquisite British wool held together to create an interesting marled effect. Finished with a softly rolled shawl collar, it's comfortable and easy to wear.

Sizes

To fit: S[M:L:XL]

To fit chest: 40–42[44–46:48–50:52–54]in (102–107[112–117:122–127:132–137]cm)

Actual chest: 45¾[48¾:52¾:56]in (116[124:134:142]cm)

Length: 29½[30¼:31:31]in (75[77:79:79]cm)

Sleeve length: 20in (51cm)

Figures in square brackets refer to larger sizes. Where only one set of figures is given, this applies to all sizes.

You will need

Erika Knight Maxi Wool 100% pure wool (approx. 87yd/80m per 100g)

8[9:9:10] x 100g hanks in Iced Gem

Erika Knight Vintage Wool 100% pure wool (approx. 95yd/87m per 50g)

8[9:9:10] x 50g hanks in Drizzle

12mm (UK–:US17) needles (using a circular needle can help to take the weight off the wrists)

Set of 12mm (UK–:US17) double-pointed needles (or circular for magic loop method)

Cable needle

Stitch markers

Stitch holders or scrap yarn

5 buttons

Note: Yarn amounts are based on average requirements and are approximate.

Tension

8 sts and 10 rows to 4in (10cm) over st st. Use larger or smaller needles if necessary to obtain the correct tension.

Abbreviations

T2R = k into the second st on the LH needle, do not slip it off, k into the first st, then slip both off the needle.

T2L = k into the second st on the LH needle tbl, do not slip it off, k into the first st, then slip both off the needle.

Cr3R = sl next st to cn and hold at back, k2, then p1 from cn.

Cr3L = sl next 2 sts to cn and hold at front, p1, then k2 from cn.

Cr5R = sl next 3 sts to cn and hold at back, k2 from LH needle, bring cn to the front, slip last st from cn back to LH needle, p1 from LH needle, k2 from cn.

Cr3L dec = (ending 1 st after 3-st cable) sl next st to RH needle, sl foll 2 sts to cn and hold at front, sl first st on RH needle back to LH needle and k tog with next st, k2 from cn.

Cr3R dec = (starting 1 st before 3-st cable) sl next st to cn and hold at back, k2, slip st from cn to RH needle, slip next st kwise, then work these two tog tbl as in ssk.

Cr5R dec RF = (ending 1 st after 5-st cable) sl3 sts to cn and hold at back, k2, sl last st from cn back to LH needle and p it, sl2 sts from cn back to LH needle, k1, ssk.

Cr5R dec LF = (starting 1 st before 5-st cable) sl next st to RH needle, sl next 3 sts to cn and hold at back, sl first st on RH needle back to LH needle, k2tog, k1, bring cn to front, slip last st on cn back to LH needle and purl it, k2 from cn.

For standard abbreviations, see page 148.

Pattern note

This cardigan is knitted in one piece to the underarm. The sleeves are worked separately, then the yoke is made all in one piece, followed by the saddle shoulder. Stitches for the button and buttonhole bands and shawl collar are picked up, and the collar is shaped by short rows.

This is probably the most complicated pattern in this book. Like all cable patterns, it may look daunting, but is in fact pretty straightforward, with plenty of stocking stitch in between simple cabled moss stitch diamond panels. If it really looks too challenging, leave out the cabling and work these stitches in stocking stitch for a plain but cosy jacket. Try casting on 2 or 3 fewer stitches as cabling comes out tighter than stocking stitch.

Diamond Moss Cable Panel

Worked over 9 sts and 10 rows:
Row 1: P2, Cr5R, p2.
Row 2: K2, p2, k1, p2, k2.
Row 3: P1, Cr3R, k1, Cr3L, p1.
Row 4: K1, p2, k1, p1, k1, p2, k1.
Row 5: Cr3R, k1, p1, k1, Cr3L.
Row 6: P2, (k1, p1) twice, k1, p2.
Row 7: Cr3L, p1, k1, p1, Cr3R.
Row 8: K1, p2, k1, p1, k1, p2, k1.
Row 9: P1, Cr3L, p1, Cr3R, p1.
Row 10: K2, p2, k1, p2, k2.

Body

With your circular needle, cast on 92[100:108:116] sts using the long tail method (see page 119).
Rib row: (K1, p1) to end.
Rep rib row 4 times. Piece measures approx. 2½in (6.5cm).

SET CABLE PANELS
Set-up row (RS): K1, p1, T2R, p1, work row 1 of Diamond Cable Panel, p1, T2L, p1, pm, k4[6:8:10], pm, k48[52:56:60], pm, k4[6:8:10], pm, p1, T2R, p1, work row 1 of Diamond Cable Panel, p1, T2L, p1, k1. You now have 22[24:26:28] sts for each Front and 48[52:56:60] sts for Back, with markers to denote cable panels.
Row 2: P1, k1, p2, k1, work row 2 of Diamond Moss Cable Panel, k1, p2, k1, sm, p to last m slipping markers in between, sm, k1, p2, k1, work row 2 of Diamond Cable Panel, k1, p2, k1, p1.
Row 3: K1, p1, k2, p1, work row 3 of Diamond Cable Panel, p1, k2, p1, sm, k to last m slipping markers in between, sm, p1, k2, p1, work row 2 of Diamond Cable Panel, p1, k2, p1, k1.
Row 4: As row 2, but working row 4 of Diamond Cable Panel.
Row 5: K1, p1, T2R, p1, work row 5 of Diamond Cable Panel, p1, T2L, p1, sm, k to last m slipping markers in between, sm, p1, T2R, p1, work row 5 of Diamond Cable Panel, p1, T2L, p1, k1.
The last four rows set the position of the Diamond Cable Panel with a twist worked on each side of each panel every fourth row. Cont in patt as set until you have worked five full reps of Diamond Cable Panel, ending with row 10. Piece measures approx. 22½in (57cm). Set aside.

Sleeves (make 2)

Cast on 20[22:24:24] sts. Join in the round, taking care not to twist sts, and pm to mark beg of round.
Round 1: (K1, p1) around.
Rep round 1 four times.
Knit 4 rounds.

SET SLEEVE SHAPING
*Next round (inc): K1, m1L, k to last st, m1R, k1.
Knit 3 rounds.
Rep from * 4[4:4:6] times, then work inc round again (32[34:36:40] sts).
Cont without shaping until Sleeve measures approx. 20in (51cm) or desired length to underarm.
Slip first and last 4[4:4:5] sts of round (8[8:8:10] sts total) to holder or scrap yarn. Set aside.

YOKE
Set-up row: Return Body sts to long circular needle and, with RS facing, work as foll: Patt 18[20:22:24] across Right front, slip 8[8:8:10] sts to holder, pm1, k across 24[26:28:30] held Sleeve sts, pm2, k across 40[44:48:50] Back sts, slip 8[8:8:10] sts to holder, pm3, k across 24[26:28:30] held Sleeve sts,

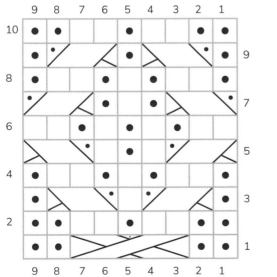

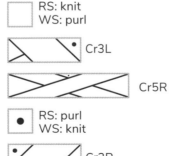

	RS: knit WS: purl								
	Cr3L								
	Cr5R								
	RS: purl WS: knit								
	Cr3R								

pm4, patt across rem 18[20:22:24] sts for Left front (124[136:148:158] sts).

Patt 7 rows as set, slipping markers and ending with row 8 of Diamond Cable Panel. Pm in a stitch at each end of last row to mark start of neck shaping.

SET YOKE DECREASES

SIZE 1 ONLY

Row 1 (RS) (dec neck and armhole): Ssk, k2, p1, work Diamond Cable Panel row 9, p1, ssk, k1, sm, k1, k2tog, *k to 3 sts before m, ssk, k1, sm, k1, k2tog; rep from * 2 more times, p1, work Diamond Cable Panel row 9, p1, k2, k2tog (114 sts).

Rows 2 and 4: Patt as set, working each st as set by cable panel or as it appears.

Row 3 (dec armhole only): K1, T2R, p1, work Diamond Cable Panel row 1, ssk, k1, sm, k1, k2tog, *k to 3 sts before marker, ssk, k1, sm, k1, k2tog; rep from * 2 more times, work Diamond Cable Panel row 1, p1, T2L, k1 (106 sts).

Row 5 (dec neck and armhole): Ssk, *work each st as it appears to 3 sts before marker, ssk, k1, sm, k1, k2tog; rep from * 3 more times, work each st as it appears to last 2 sts, k2tog (96 sts).

Row 6 and all foll alt rows: Work each st as it appears.

Row 7 (dec armhole only): (Work each st as it appears to 3 sts before marker, ssk, k1, sm, k1, k2tog) 4 times, work each st as it appears to end (88 sts).

Rows 9–16: As rows 5–8 (52 sts).

SIZE 2 ONLY

Row 1 (RS) (dec neck and armhole): Ssk, k2, p1, work Diamond Cable Panel row 9, p1, k1, ssk, k1, sm, k1, k2tog, *k to 3 sts before marker, ssk, k1, sm, k1, k2tog; rep from * 2 more times, p1, work Diamond Cable Panel row 9, p1, k2, k2tog (126 sts).

Row 2 and all foll alt rows: Patt as set, working each st as set by cable panel or as it appears.

Row 3 (dec armhole only): K1, T2R, p1, work Diamond Cable Panel row 1, p1, k1, ssk, k1, sm, k1, k2tog, *k to 3 sts before marker, ssk, k1, sm, k1, k2tog; rep from * 2 more times, k1, p1, work Diamond Cable Panel row 1, p1, T2L, k1 (118 sts).

Row 5 (dec neck and armhole): Ssk, k1, p1, work Diamond Cable Panel row 3, p1, ssk, k1, sm, k1, k2tog, *k to 3 sts before marker, ssk, k1, sm, k1, k2tog; rep from * 2 more times, p1, work Diamond Cable Panel row 3, p1, k1, k2tog (108 sts).

Row 7 (dec armhole only): K2, p1, work Diamond Cable Panel row 5, ssk, k1, sm, k1, k2tog, *k to 3 sts before marker, ssk, k1, sm, k1, k2tog; rep from * 2 more times, work Diamond Cable Panel row 5, p1, k2 (100 sts).

Row 9 (dec neck and armhole):

Ssk, p1, Cr3L, p1, k1, p1, Cr3R dec, k1, sm, k1, k2tog, *k to 3 sts before marker, ssk, k1, sm, k1, k2tog; rep from * once more, k to 3 sts before marker, ssk, k1, sm, k1, Cr3L dec, p1, k1, p1, Cr3R, p1, k2tog (90 sts).

Row 11 (dec armhole only): K1, p2, Cr3L, p1, Cr3R dec, k1, sm, k1, k2tog, *k to 3 sts before marker, ssk, k1, sm, k1, k2tog; rep from * once more, k to 3 sts before marker, ssk, k1, sm, k1, Cr3L dec, p1, Cr3R, p2, k1 (82 sts).

Row 13 (dec neck and armhole): Ssk, p2, Cr5R dec RF, k1, sm, k1, k2tog, *k to 3 sts before marker, ssk, k1, sm, k1, k2tog; rep from * once, k to 3 sts before marker, ssk, k1, sm, k1, Cr5R dec LF, p2, k2tog (72 sts).

Row 15 (dec armhole only): K1, work each st as it appears to 3 sts before marker, ssk, k1, sm, k1, k2tog, *k to 3 sts before marker, ssk, k1, sm, k1, k2tog; rep from * 2 more times, work each st as it appears to last st, k1.

Row 17 (dec neck and armhole): Ssk, work each st as it appears to 3 sts before marker, ssk, k1, sm, k1, k2tog, *k to 3 sts before marker, ssk, k1, sm, k1, k2tog; rep from * 2 more times, work each st as it appears to last 2 sts, k2tog (54 sts).

Row 18 (WS): Work each st as it appears.

SIZES 3 AND 4 ONLY

Note: Read all of next section before continuing.

Cont in patt as set to end of current Diamond Cable Panel and for one more full 10-row patt rep, noting that decs will eat into the twists on either side of the Diamond Cable Panel. When there are no longer enough sts to work the twist, work each st as it appears. AT THE SAME TIME, dec as foll:

Row 1 (RS) (dec neck and armhole): Ssk, patt to 3 sts before marker, ssk, k1, sm, k1, sm, k2tog; rep from * 3 more times, patt to last 2 sts, k2tog (dec 10).

Rows 2 and 4 (WS): Work each st as set by Diamond Cable Panel or as it appears.

Row 3 (dec armhole only): Patt to 3 sts before marker, ssk, k1, sm, k1, k2tog; rep from * 3 more times, patt to end (dec 8).

Rep these 4 rows twice more, ending with row 10 of Diamond Cable Panel.

At the end of the Diamond Cable Panel you will have 94[104] sts.

SIZE 3 ONLY

Next row (RS) (dec neck and armhole): Ssk, p2, Cr5R, p1, ssk, k1, sm, k1, k2tog, *k to 3 sts before marker, ssk, k1, sm, k1, k2tog; rep from * 2 more times, p1, Cr5R, p2, k2tog (84 sts).

SIZE 4 ONLY

Next row (RS) (dec neck and armhole): Ssk, work Diamond Cable Panel row 1, p1, ssk, k1, sm, k1, k2tog, *k to 3 sts before marker, ssk, k1, sm, k1, k2tog; rep from * 2 more times, p1, work Diamond Cable Panel row 1, k2tog (94 sts).

SIZES 3 AND 4 ONLY

Next and all foll alt rows (WS): Work each st as it appears.

Next row (RS) (dec armhole only): *Work each st as it appears to 3 sts before marker, ssk, k1, sm, k1, k2tog; rep from * 3 more times, work each st as it appears to end (76[86] sts).

Next RS row (dec neck and armhole): Ssk, *work each st as it appears to 3 sts before marker, ssk, k1, sm, k1, k2tog; rep from * 3 more times, work each st as it appears to last 2 sts, k2tog. (66[76] sts)

Next RS row: Work armhole dec row once more (58[68] sts).

Work one more alt row.

ALL SIZES

52[54:58:68] sts: 6[6:7:9] sts for each Front, 8[8:8:10] sts for each Sleeve, 24[26:28:30] sts for Back. Pm at centre of Back sts.

SHAPE SADDLE SHOULDER
RIGHT SHOULDER

Row 1 (RS): K to m1, sm, sl1, k to last st before next marker, ssk (last Sleeve st with first Back st), turn.

Row 2: Sl1, p6[6:6:8], p2tog (last Sleeve st with first Front st), turn.

Row 3: Sl1, k6[6:6:8], ssk, turn.

Rep rows 2 and 3 until all sts of Right Front have been worked, ending with a WS row.

Next row: Cast off 4[4:4:5] sts, k to last Sleeve st, ssk (last Sleeve st tog with first Back st), turn.

Next row: Sl1, p to end.

Next row: K to last Sleeve st, ssk (last Sleeve st tog with first Back st), turn.

Rep last 2 rows until you reach centre Back marker.

Next row (WS): P to end.

Leave rem 4[4:4:5] sts on a holder.

LEFT SHOULDER

With WS facing, rejoin working yarn to Left front edge.

Row 1 (WS): P to marker, sm, sl1, p to last st before next marker, p2tog (last Sleeve st with first Back st), turn.

Row 2: Sl1, k6[6:6:8], ssk (last Sleeve st with first Front st), turn.

Row 3: Sl1, p6[6:6:8], p2tog, turn.

Rep rows 2 and 3 until all sts of Left front have been worked, ending with a RS row.

Next row: Cast off 4[4:4:5] sts pwise, p to last Sleeve st, p2tog (last Sleeve st tog with first Back st, turn.

Next row (RS): K to end.

Next row: P to last Sleeve st, p2tog (last Sleeve st tog with first Back st), turn.

Rep last 2 rows until you reach centre Back.

Leave 4[4:4:5] rem Sleeve sts on a holder.

Graft rem sts from each side of saddle using Kitchener stitch (see page 138).

Interim make-up

Slip both sets of underarm sts for Right sleeve back to two needles and join using Kitchener stitch. Rep for Left sleeve. Weave in ends.

Shawl collar

With RS facing, starting at bottom edge of Right front, pick up and knit 43 stitches up Right front, pm, pick up and knit 25[27:27:29] sts to centre Back marker, pm, pick up and knit 25[27:27:29] sts to end of neck shaping, pm, pick up and knit 43 sts along Left front (136[140:140:144] sts).

Rib row (WS): (K1, p1) to end.

Rep rib row 2 more times.
Next row (RS): Rib to last marker (start of neck shaping), w&t.
Short row 1: Rib to 1 st before last m (start of neck shaping), w&t.
Short row 2: Rib to 5 sts before wrapped st, w&t.
Short row 3: Rib to 5 sts before wrapped st, w&t.
Rep rows 2 and 3 two more times, rib to end working wraps tog with wrapped sts as you come to them.

Next row (WS) (buttonholes): Rib 2, (yo, p2tog, rib 6) 4 times, yo, p2tog, rib to end working rem wraps tog with wrapped sts as you come to them.
Rib 3 more rows.
Cast off in rib.

To finish

Weave in rem ends. Sew on buttons to match buttonholes. Pin to measurements, cover with damp cloths and leave to dry.

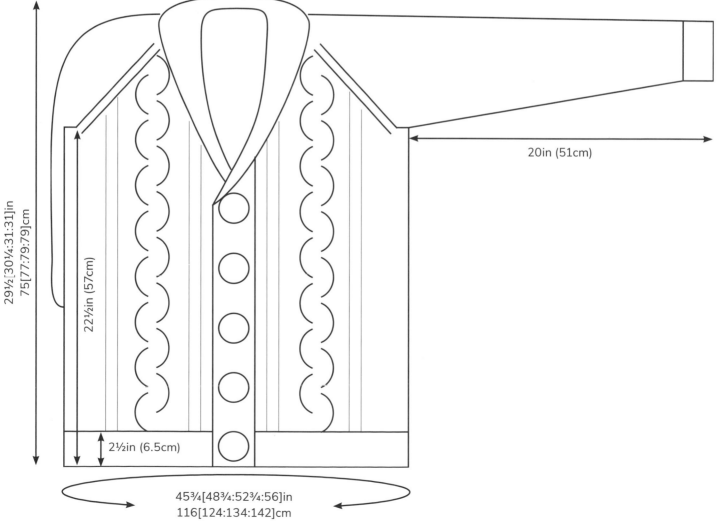

20in (51cm)

29½[30¼:31:31]in
75[77:79:79]cm

22½in (57cm)

2½in (6.5cm)

45¾[48¾:53¾:56]in
116[124:134:142]cm

End of the rainbow

It can be hard to knit for new arrivals, especially if you don't know which variety it is going to be. But rainbows suit everyone, and this ultra-simple garter stitch blanket is perfect for keeping any baby snuggled up. It is great for beginners, too, as all you do is knit. The edging is crocheted on in two easy stitch types.

Size

To fit: Car seat or Moses basket
Width: Approx. 21¾in (55cm)
Length: Approx. 29¼in (74cm)
Note: This fabric is very stretchy, so measurements are approximate. The same yarn amounts would be enough to make a slightly larger blanket if you prefer. Simply cast on a few extra stitches and knit a few extra rows in each stripe.

You will need

Cascade Yarns 128 Superwash 100% superwash Merino wool (approx. 128yd/117m per 100g)
1 x 100g hank each in:
809 Really Red (A)
822 Pumpkin (B)
820 Lemon (C)
235 Ivy (D)
896 Blue Horizon (E)
1959 Deep Sapphire (F)
1965 Dark Plum (G)
817 Ecru (H)
6.5mm (UK3:US10½) needles
6mm (UK4:USJ/10) crochet hook
Note: Yarn amounts given are based on average requirements and are approximate.

Tension

12 sts and 26 rows to 4in (10cm). Use larger or smaller needles if necessary to obtain the correct tension.

Abbreviations

See page 148.

Blanket

Cast on 60 sts in A.
Knit 26 rows.
*Change to B.
Knit 26 rows.
Rep from * but with C, D, E, F and G.
Cast off.
Weave in ends neatly on WS.

EDGING

Starting at bottom (G) LH corner, with crochet hook and H, work *3dc in corner, 1dc in each st along short edge, 3dc in corner, 1dc between each g st ridge along side edge; rep from * and join with a sl st.

Next round: 2ch (counts as first htr), 4 more htr in corner st, *1htr in each dc along edge, 5htr in corner; rep from * to end of round, join with a sl st and fasten off.

To finish

Weave in rem ends.
Block if required.

Walking on rainbows

These teeny-weeny rainbow booties to keep tiny toes toasty are cute and very quick to make. They are ideal for a last-minute gift that you can knit up on the train or bus on your way to meet the new arrival.

Size

To fit: Newborn[0–6:6–12:12–18] months

Leg circumference: Approx. 4[4:4¼:4¾]in (10[10:11:12]cm)

Foot length: Approx. 3[3½:4:4¼]in (7.5[9:10:11]cm)

Figures in square brackets refer to larger sizes. Where only one set of figures is given, this applies to all sizes.

You will need

Cascade Yarns 128 Superwash 100% superwash Merino wool (approx. 128yd/117m per 100g)

1 x 100g hank in 817 Ecru (A)

Small amounts in each of:

1965 Dark Plum (B)

1959 Deep Sapphire (C)

896 Blue Horizon (D)

235 Ivy (E)

820 Lemon (F)

822 Pumpkin (G)

809 Really Red (H)

4.5mm (UK7:US7) double-pointed or circular needles (for magic loop method)

Stitch marker

Note: Yarn amounts given are based on average requirements and are approximate.

Tension

20 sts and 26 rows to 4in (10cm). Use larger or smaller needles if necessary to obtain the correct tension.

Abbreviations

See page 148.

Bootie (make 2)

Cast on 8[8:10:12] sts in A using Judy's magic cast-on (see page 121). Pm to mark beg of round.

Round 1: *Kfb, k2[2:3:4], kfb; rep from * to end (12[12:14:16] sts).

Round 2: Knit.

Round 3: *Kfb, k4[4:5:6], kfb; rep from * to end (16[16:18:20] sts).

Knit 2[4:5:2] rounds.

SET RAINBOW PATTERN
SIZES 1 TO 3 ONLY

Round 1: K1 in A, k6 in B, k to end in A.

Rep round 1 six times, but using C, D, E, F, G and H in turn instead of B.

SIZE 4 ONLY

Rounds 1 and 2: K2 in A, k6 in B, k to end in A.

Rep rounds 1 and 2 six times, but using C, D, E, F, G and H in turn instead of B.

ALL SIZES

Break all other colours and cont in A only.

Knit 1[3:4:2] rounds.

TURN HEEL

Short row 1: K to last st, w&t.

Short row 2: P6[6:7:8], w&t.

Short row 3: K to st before wrapped st, w&t.

Short row 4: P to st before wrapped st, w&t.

Rep rows 3 and 4 until 4[4:5:6] sts remain unwrapped.

Next row: K to first wrapped st, k wrap tog with wrapped st, turn.

Next row: P to first wrapped st, p wrap tog with wrapped st, turn.

Rep last 2 rows until all wrapped sts have been worked, then k to end of round.

LEG

Rib round: (K1, p1) around.

Rep rib round until leg measures approx. 1½[1¾:2:2¼]in (4[4.5:5:5.5]cm).

Cast off loosely in rib.

To finish

Weave in the ends. You may wish to weave in the coloured ends before working the heel turn as the many ends can be bulky, especially in the tiniest sizes. Make sure your stitches are secure before doing this so that you don't drop any.

Warm heart

Cables can look complicated but are in fact surprisingly simple. This quick-to-knit beanie with an eye-catching cable heart motif will warm your head while your pride in your new skills can make you feel warm inside.

Size
To fit: Average adult
Circumference:
    Approx. 19¾in (50cm)
Depth: 9¾in (25cm)

You will need
Wool and the Gang Crazy Sexy
    Wool 100% wool
    (approx. 87yd/80m per 200g)
1 x 200g ball in Bronzed Olive
OR Wool and the Gang Heal The
    Wool 100% recycled wool
    (approx. 87yd/80m per 200g)
1 x 200g ball in Midnight Blue
12mm (UK–:US17) double-pointed
    or circular needles
Cable needle
Stitch marker
Pompom maker (optional)
Note: Yarn amounts given are
based on average requirements
and are approximate.

Tension
7 sts and 10 rounds to 4in (10cm).
Use larger or smaller needles
if necessary to obtain the
correct tension.

Abbreviations
Cr5R = Slip 3 sts to cn and hold at
back of work, k2, slip last st from cn
back to LH needle, p1,
k2 from cn.
Cr2R = Sl1 st to cn and hold at back,
k2, p1 from cn.
Cr2L = Sl2 sts to cn and hold at
front, p1, k2 from cn.
For standard abbreviations,
see page 148.

Warm heart pattern

Worked over 18 sts and 13 rounds.

Round 1: P6, k2, p1, k2, p7.
Round 2: P6, Cr5R, p7.
Round 3: Rep round 1.
Round 4: P5, Cr2R, k1, Cr2L, p6.
Round 5: P5, k2, p1, k1, p1, k2, p6.
Round 6: P4, Cr2R, k1, p1, k1, Cr2L, p5.
Round 7: P4, k2, (p1, k1) twice, p1, k2, p5.
Round 8: P3, Cr2R, (k1, p1) twice, k1, Cr2L, p4.
Round 9: P3, k2, (p1, k1) 3 times, p1, k2, p4.
Round 10: P3, Cr2L, Cr5R, Cr2R, p4.
Round 11: P4, k4, p1, k4, p5.
Round 12: P5, k3, p1, k3, p6.
Round 13: Purl.

Hat

Cast on 36 sts. Join in the round, taking care not to twist sts, and pm to mark beg of round.
Round 1: (P2, k2) around.
Rep round 1 3 more times.

SET WARM HEART PATTERN
Rounds 1–13: Work 18-st cable panel twice around.

SET DECREASE PATTERN
Round 1: (P4, p2tog) around (30 sts).
Rounds 2 and 4: Purl.
Round 3: (P3, p2tog) around (24 sts).
Round 5: (P2, p2tog) around (18 sts).
Round 6: (P1, p2tog) around (12 sts).
Round 7: (P2tog) around (6 sts).
Break yarn, thread through rem 6 sts and pull tight to fasten off.

To finish

Weave in ends neatly. Block if required. Make a big pompom (see page 147) and fasten to top of hat.

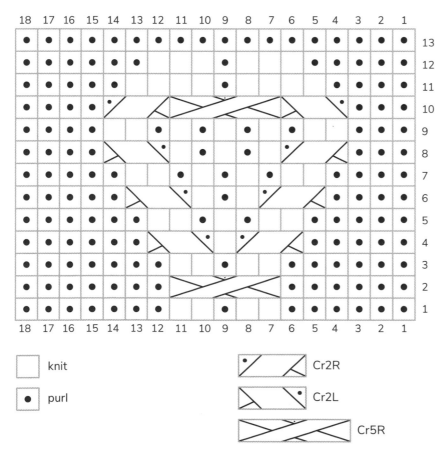

	knit
•	purl

Cr2R	
Cr2L	
Cr5R	

Find your tribe

If you've fallen in love with knitting but don't have anyone to share your newfound passion, don't despair! Avid knitters are everywhere and the easiest place to find them is online. There are many moving stories of lifelong friendships based on common interests that are made online before being cemented in real life, so don't be afraid to click on down and seek out fellow crafters.

YARN SHOPS

If you're not keen on ones and zeros, look for some fellow knitters in your area. The best place to seek them out is at a local yarn shop. Many run classes or knit nights where you will find like-minded crafters you can connect with in the real world.

RAVELRY

The knitters' and crocheters' network Ravelry is an exhaustive database of amazing patterns as well as a place for crafters to meet and share their passions. With options to join groups, swap your stash with others and so much more, Ravelry is the place to be.

INSTAGRAM

Knitters love to post their works in progress (WIPs) and finished items and to comment on each others' achievements. Exciting independent businesses also show their wares on the network.

PINTEREST

Sharing inspiration or your finished project by pinning pictures is a great way to get in touch with like-minded people.

FACEBOOK

There are plenty of knitters and knitting-related businesses to find on the social network.

TWITTER

Used much like Instagram but without the focus on photos, Twitter is great for sharing WIPs, finished objects and opinions.

GOOGLE

The best site to help you seek out your local yarn shop and start meeting knitters in person.

Lovely bobbly

These cute brioche-stitch hats are reversible and are completed with mix-and-match pompoms for extra fun. They are sized so that all the family can wear one, and they make a great quick knit if you need a gift in a hurry.

Size

To fit: Child age 5–10[age 11–small adult:large adult]
Actual brim circumference: 14[15¾:17¼]in (36[40:44]cm) but very stretchy
Depth: 8¼[9:9¾]in (21[23:24.5]cm)
Figures in square brackets refer to larger sizes. Where only one set of figures is given, this refers to all sizes.

You will need

Rico Essentials Super Super Chunky 50% acrylic, 50% wool (approx. 109yd/100m per 100g)
All sizes: 1 x 100g ball each in shade A and shade B
Samples knitted in:
Size 1: 22 Lilac (A) and 01 Cream (B)
Size 2: 33 Dark Blue (A) and 30 Pale Blue (B) or 01 Cream (A) and 11 Dark Pink (B)
Size 3: 27 Silver Grey (A) and 30 Pale Blue (B)
10mm (UK000:US15) double-pointed or circular needles
Stitch marker
4 x 1³⁄₁₆in (30mm) press studs
Note: Yarn amounts are based on average requirements and are approximate.

Tension

9 sts and 15 rows to 4in (10cm) over 1 x 1 rib.
7 sts and 20 rows to 4in (10cm) over two-colour brioche. Use larger or smaller needles if necessary to obtain the correct tension.

Abbreviations

See page 148.

Pattern note

Refer to page 133 for more instructions on brioche knitting.

Hat

Using A, cast on 32[36:40] sts. Join in the round, taking care not to twist stitches, and pm to mark beg of round.
Rib round: (K1, p1) around.
Rep rib round 2[3:3] times.
SET TWO-COLOUR BRIOCHE
Set-up round 1: Using A, (k1, sl1yo) around.
Set-up round 2: Join B at the back, then bring yarn to the front and work (sl1yo, brp1) around.
Round 1: With A (brk1, sl1yo) around.
Round 2: With B (sl1yo, brp1) around.
Rep these 2 rounds 13[17:19] more times, ending with round 2. Break B and cont in A only.

Next round: (Brk1, p1) around.
SHAPE CROWN
SIZES 1 AND 3 ONLY
Round 1: *Sk2po, p1, (k1, p1) 2[3] times; rep from * 4 times (24[32] sts).
Rounds 2 and 4: Rib as set.
Round 3: (Sk2po, p1) around (12[16] sts).
Round 5: (Sk2po, p1) to end (6[8] sts).
SHAPE CROWN SIZE 2 ONLY
Round 1: *Sk2po, p1, (k1, p1) twice; rep from * 4 times, (k1, p1) twice (28 sts).
Rounds 2 and 4: Rib as set.
Round 3: (Sk2po, p1) around (14 sts).
Round 5: (Sk2po, p1) to last 2 sts, skpo (7 sts).
ALL SIZES
Thread yarn through rem sts and pull tight to secure.

To finish

Weave in ends very neatly. Make two pompoms (see page 147), one in A and one in B. Sew one side of a press stud to point of hat on both sides. Sew the corresponding side of the press studs on to each pompom.

Mittens dressed up as lamb

I can't resist a pun, and I can't resist these chunky mittens showing sheep grazing in green fields either. They fit kids and adults and are quick to knit in one colour. The fluffy sheep motif is embroidered or Swiss darned on at the end.

Size
To fit: Child age 5–10[Adult]
Finished hand circumference:
    7[9]in (18[23]cm)
Finished length: 8[10¼]in (20[26]cm)

Figures in square brackets refer to larger sizes. Where only one set of figures is given, this applies to all sizes.

You will need
Erika Knight Maxi Wool 100% pure
    British wool (approx. 87yd/80m
    per 100g)
1[1] x 100g hank in 206 Artisan
Erika Knight Fat Fur Wool 97% pure
    British wool, 3% nylon (approx.
    44yd/40m per 100g)
Small amount in 001 Flax
Black embroidery thread
10mm (UK000:US15) double-
    pointed or circular needles
Stitch holder
Stitch markers
Large-eyed, blunt-ended needle
Note: Yarn amounts given are based
on average requirements and are
approximate.

Tension
9 sts and 15 rows to 4in (10cm)
over st st.
Use larger or smaller needles
if necessary to obtain the
correct tension.

Abbreviations
See page 148.

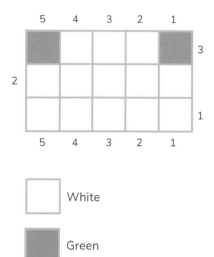

	5	4	3	2	1	
	Green	White	White	White	Green	3
2	White	White	White	White	White	
	White	White	White	White	White	1
	5	4	3	2	1	

□ White

■ Green

Left mitten

Cast on 12[16] sts. Join to work in the round, taking care not to twist sts, and pm to mark beg of round.

Rib round: (K1, p1) around.

Rep rib round 4[7] more times.

Next round (inc): *K1, kfb, k2[4], kfb, k1; rep from * to end (16[20] sts).

Knit 7[12] rounds.**

SET THUMBHOLE

Next round: K6, slip 2[3] sts to holder, cast on 2[3] sts, k to end.

***Knit 11[14] rounds or desired length to top of ring finger.

SHAPE TOP

Next round (dec): *K1, ssk, k2[4], k2tog, k1; rep from * once (12[16] sts).

Next round (dec): *K1, ssk, k0[2], k2tog, k1; rep from * once (8[12] sts).

Divide rem 8[12] sts equally over two dpns or the tips of the circular needle and join using Kitchener st (see page 138).

Right mitten

Work as for Left mitten to **.

SET THUMBHOLE

Next round: Slip 2[3] sts to holder, cast on 2[3] sts, k to end.

Work as for Left mitten from *** to end.

Thumb (both alike)

Slip 2[3] sts from holder to needle, pick up and knit 1 st from side of thumbhole, 2[3] sts across cast-on sts and 1 st from other side of thumbhole (6[8] sts).

Knit 5[8] rounds.

Next round (dec): (K2tog) around (3[4] sts).

Break yarn and thread through rem sts, pull tight to secure.

Sheep motif

Position Chart 5[10] sts down from mitten top, 1[2] sts from thumb side of mitten.

Embroider sheep pattern in this position from the chart using Swiss darning or duplicate stitch (see page 147). Add a head and legs in black embroidery thread.

To finish

Weave in ends.

5 life lessons I've learned from knitting

I knit a lot, and I've knitted a lot for a long time, without really thinking about how my craft has affected me. But a recent conversation made me take stock. I realized that, in some respects, my whole outlook has been changed by lessons I've learned from knitting.

1

YOU CAN GO YOUR OWN WAY

I've never been very good at following patterns. If I do follow one, I'll find the back and sleeves are too short, so I have to adjust them anyway. Apart from that, I might not like the suggested yarn, or the motif, or a certain texture. And that's fine! I can adapt these things and make the project all my own. That means the end result is even better, because it's completely unique.

2

WHAT YOU WANT TO KNIT ISN'T ALWAYS WHAT YOU WANT TO WEAR

I'm a bit contrary when it comes to fashion. Sometimes I'll go for weeks decked out in the boldest colours: fuchsia, yellow, turquoise, orange and olive green. At other times, I wear nothing but greys and blacks. I'm always thinking I'd like to knit a super-soft wardrobe staple in black – but I can't do it. I just can't face spending day after day knitting in black. So I've resigned myself to buying the odd jumper in a colour I really want to wear, and knitting in as many beautiful brights as I can manage.

3

YOU DON'T ALWAYS HAVE TO FINISH

Some people are able to pick up a book, start watching a TV series or start a project and, if they don't get on with it, simply let it go. That's not me. I've always felt the need to finish, gritting my teeth through things I couldn't stand, including *Vanity Fair* by William Thackeray, *Biographia Literaria* by Samuel Taylor Coleridge (which was thrown out of the window more than once when studying it at university) and season seven of *The Vampire Diaries*. Knitting has helped me understand that I don't have to waste my time on these things. If I'm not enjoying a project, I can set it aside and try something else. I may come back to it; I may not. Or it may become something different. It's all good.

4

GO SLOWLY AND GET IT RIGHT

Perfectionism has become something of a dirty word recently. Many people struggle with a constant, futile drive towards perfectionism – but that's never been my problem. As a journalist, I'm all about doing something quickly and getting it right. Anything that meets those two criteria is good enough; anything more is a bonus. When I first started knitting I took the same attitude to my craft, making all sorts of speed errors and correcting them with fudges that I hoped no one would notice. It is only recently that I have come to appreciate the potential for perfection in knitting. These days I'm happy to keep ripping something back until I get it right.

5

IT'S ALL ABOUT THE JOURNEY

You may have come across the terms 'process knitter' and 'product knitter' before. In a sense, I'll always be a product knitter: the practical part of me wants to work on something useful. But the more I knit, the more I enjoy it simply for the knitting – it's my inner process knitter coming out.

You don't need much to get started with knitting – it's all about sticks and string! In the following pages you'll find some of the key kit and useful skills to get you going.

Tools and Techniques

Tools of the trade

The great thing about knitting is that it doesn't need a great deal of equipment. You won't need to build a studio, invest in heavy machinery or buy a special outfit. However, there are a few basic things you will need.

Needles
There are several types of knitting needle available. If you're just starting out, it's worth trying out a few to see which you like best.

STRAIGHT NEEDLES (3)
This is the traditional knitting needle and is still preferred by many knitters worldwide. Straight needles come in many materials, from plastic and wood to metal and even carbon fibre – the material used to build racing cars. Metal needles can be more slippery than plastic or wood; this can be a benefit if you're a tight knitter or a problem if your tension tends to be loose. Experiment with a few different types, and don't be surprised if what you like changes over time. Until a year ago I was a die-hard fan of metal needles, then I suddenly went all out for wood.

CIRCULAR NEEDLES (4)
Circular needles are two needle tips linked by a flexible cord. Like straight needles, these come in all different materials, and the thickness and suppleness of the cord varies from brand to brand. Circular needles come in a range of different lengths, either as fixed needles or in interchangeable sets, where needle tips can be mixed and matched with different length cords.

Circulars are my favourites. I particularly recommend them for the projects in this book, as many of them have large numbers of stitches and use chunky yarns, which can be heavy. Circular needles allow the weight of the knitting to sit in your lap rather than hanging from your wrist, which can protect against strain.

The other good thing about circular needles is that you can use them either to knit flat or in the round. The magic loop method (see page 128) allows you to knit any circumference of knitting with the same needles.

DOUBLE-POINTED NEEDLES (2)
Double-pointed needles (dpns) are generally used for small-circumference knitting in the round, such as socks or sleeves. Circular needle fans can use the magic loop method instead (see page 128), but dpns allow for smoother working, without adjusting your knitting twice every round. Dpns are short needles with a point at each end. They usually come in sets of four or five, so you can divide your stitches over three or four needles and use the last one to work with.

CABLE NEEDLES (5)
Used for cabling, these are short, double-pointed needles with a hooked section, ridges or notches to stop the stitches slipping. If you don't have a cable needle, you could use a double-pointed one to achieve the same effect.

OTHER NEEDLE TYPES
There are many other ways to work knitted fabric. In Scotland, long double-pointed needles, worked with a knitting belt, are popular. There's no reason why you shouldn't knit the projects in this book using a knitting belt, or any other method that works for you.

Stitch holders (8)
Occasionally you will be asked to slip stitches to a holder to keep them out of the way while a different section is worked before returning them to the needles to knit. Stitch holders that look like over-sized safety pins are available and can be really useful, but are not essential. Scrap yarn and actual safety pins are good alternatives.

Scissors (7)
Every knitter needs a good pair of scissors for cutting yarn and trimming ends. You don't need a large pair; a pair you can slip into your bag and take with you anywhere is ideal. I've tried lots of types; my favourite is a small pair of embroidery scissors.

Yarn needles (6)

You will need a large-eyed, blunt-ended needle to sew pieces of fabric together and weave in yarn ends.

Measuring tape (10)

A good flexible one is a must.

Optional extras

There are many optional extras you might fancy as you get into knitting: beautiful project bags are my weakness, but there are also needle cases, yarn bowls, stash baskets and much more. None of them are essential, but all of them are lovely. Indulge if you wish, refrain if you don't: the knitting world is your oyster.

Crochet hooks (1)

Like knitting needles, crochet hooks come in all shapes, sizes and materials. I have a set made of sparkly resin. They aren't the easiest to work with but they look amazing, so I persevere! You will need a crochet hook for some of the projects in this book. They're also handy for picking up dropped stitches, so I recommend investing in one or two.

Stitch markers (9)

Stitch markers can be anything from scrap yarn or safety pins to bespoke handmade beauties (see page 76). Two types are used in this book. The first are markers that denote different sections of the design – for instance, the point where the back meets the sleeve in a jumper. When the instructions ask you to place a marker (pm), simply slip the marker onto the needle in between stitches at this point. When you next come to the marker, slip it from needle to needle as instructed. The second type of markers are ones that can be placed in actual stitches to mark a point in the fabric to which you may need to return.

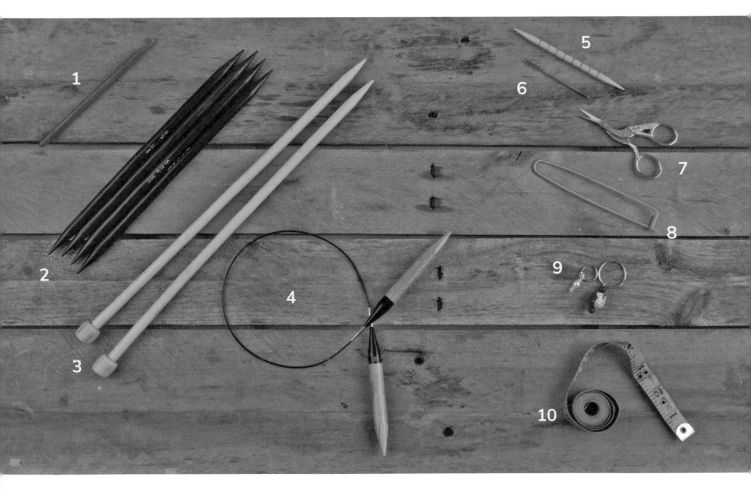

A yarn to spin

Yarn can be made from all sorts of materials, from wool and cotton to nettle fibre and corn. Here is a brief introduction.

Wool

Wool is the most common fibre used in yarn. Some knitters refer to any type of yarn as 'wool', but the primary definition of wool is fleece shorn from a sheep and spun into a yarn you can knit with. Wool can be as firm and sturdy as a Harris Tweed jacket or as soft and delicate as cashmere (which actually comes from the undercoats of angora goats). Merino is a particularly soft wool that is popular in chunky yarns, and there is plenty of lovely merino in this book. If you've felt uncomfortable in woollen garments before, I would recommend trying a small project in merino; it may be softer than you imagine.

Cotton

Cotton is a popular knitting fibre made from the cotton plant. I find it quite hard to work with, so there are no cotton yarns in this book, but some crafters love working with this cool, soft and flexible fibre.

Alpaca

Alpacas provide beautifully soft fibre that can be extremely warm and lovely to work with. Llama yarn is less well known than alpaca, but just as deliciously soft.

Artificial fibres

Synthetic fibres such as nylon, acrylic and polyester can make stand-alone yarns or be used in blends with natural fibres to create a stronger yarn. They are generally made from petroleum-derived chemicals and won't biodegrade, but on the plus side they are less appealing to moths and other wool predators than natural fibres. Some synthetic fibres such as rayon and viscose are made from plant-based materials.

IS THIS A WIND-UP?

Some yarns come in round balls, oval skeins or cylindrical 'cakes' that are ready to knit straight away. Just find the end and you're ready to go. A useful tip is that if you find the end that starts at the centre of the ball, the yarn will roll about less as you work.

Others – and this is true of a number of projects in this book – come in hank form, which means long loops of yarn that need to be wound before you work with them. DO NOT try to skip this step: you are likely to end up in a terrible tangle if you do.

I wind a lot of yarn, so I have invested in a swift – which looks a bit like the inside of an umbrella that stands alone or screws onto a table top – and a ball winder, which turns my hanks into neat cakes. Neither was very expensive, and they have made my knitting life much easier. However, they aren't essential and you can certainly manage without if you prefer.

How to wind yarn

Carefully open your hank out into a single big loop. Place it over your swift or, if you don't have one, the backs of two straight-backed chairs set back to back a little apart from each other.

Make sure the hank is lying completely smoothly with no twists, then carefully cut the ties holding the hank in place and find the end of the yarn.

If you are using a ball winder, attach the end to the mechanism, then carefully begin unwinding the yarn from the hank and turning the ball winder to wind it up again.

To wind the yarn into a ball, pinch the yarn end between the thumb and forefinger of your left hand and begin winding it around the outside of those two fingers.

Once you have done a few loops, slip these off the thumb and forefinger and wind the yarn around the ball you have created. Always hold one finger underneath the yarn you are winding to stop the ball becoming too tight.

Keep changing the angle at which you are winding the yarn so that you end up with a neat, round ball.

Before you begin

It's exciting to plunge headlong into a new project, but there are a few steps you should take first to make sure your project comes out the way you intend.

Taking measurements

The key measurement in these designs is the bust or chest measurement. The measurement should be taken across the full bust. Compare your size (or the size of the person you're knitting for) with both the size the garment is intended for (the 'to fit' size) and the actual size of the finished garment. Many of the garments are intended to be oversized and slouchy, and have a lot of what is called positive ease – this means they will be bigger than your actual bust. If you're concerned the garment may be too bulky, try a smaller size than normal. In other patterns you may find a garment with an actual measurement smaller than your bust size. This is called negative ease; it means the garment will be close-fitting and will stretch to fit.

Other key measurements are the length of the garment, which should be measured from the back neck, and the sleeve length, measured from underarm to wrist.

Both full lengths and sleeve lengths are fairly easy to adjust. Simply find a section that is worked straight and add or subtract the number of rows or rounds that will make it the right length for you. If you are working a stitch pattern you will need to add in or subtract a full pattern repeat.

A note on sleeves: I love a long sleeve that will hang right over my hands and keep them warm, so the patterns in this book are designed with this in mind. If you prefer a shorter sleeve, I advise measuring your arm, taking note of the length you require, and knitting to suit yourself. Most sleeve instructions ask you to knit to a certain length or the length you want – this is the point at which to make any adjustments.

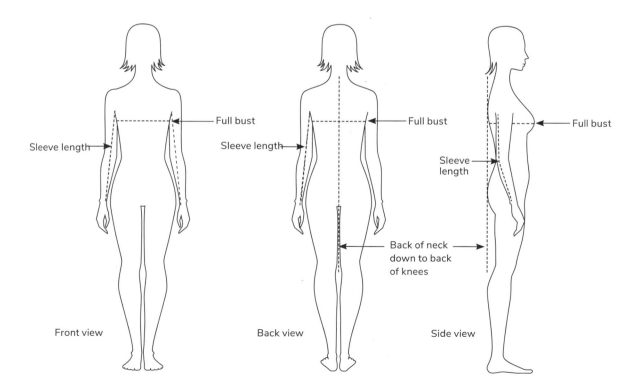

Full bust

Sleeve length

Front view

Full bust

Sleeve length

Back of neck down to back of knees

Back view

Full bust

Sleeve length

Side view

HOW TO KNIT A TENSION SQUARE

There are lots of ways to knit a tension square. The main idea is to knit something slightly bigger than the 4 x 4in (10 x 10cm) square you need to measure so that you can measure the square at a few different points. Most books recommend knitting a square of 6 x 6in (15 x 15cm) or even 8 x 8in (20 x 20cm), but some ingenious designers have come up with more fun ideas. Tin Can Knits recommends knitting tension triangles that can eventually be threaded together to make bunting, while *A Stash of One's Own* author Clara Parkes knits her swatches into mittens. You can find both these designs on ravelry.com.

Once you have knitted your swatch, use a measuring tape or a ruler and a needle to count how many stitches and rows you have per 4in (10cm). If these match up with the designer's, you're good to go. If you have too many stitches or rows, try bigger needles. If you have too few, try smaller ones. You may have to knit a few squares (or triangles, or mitts) before you get it right, but it's better to discover this at the start of a project than at the end, when you find that instead of the cute sweater you wanted, you've knitted something only a doll could wear – or a full-size family tent.

Knitting a tension square

WHY KNIT A TENSION SQUARE?

Every knitting book or magazine will beg you to please, please, please knit a tension square – and this one is no exception. It may seem tedious, but you can learn a lot from a tension square:

1 Whether your finished item will turn out the same size as the designer's. If your tension matches the designer's in a square, it should match in the finished garment. This is not always 100% true, but it is a good guide.

2 Whether the recommended needle size and yarn work together for you. You may not like the texture of the fabric when it's knitted on the recommended needle size, in which case you should experiment with other sizes until you find one you're happy with.

3 What the fabric will actually look like. Photos lie – they never look exactly like real life. A tension square will show you what you will really end up with. If you hate it, you may want to use the yarn for something else. If you love it, you've got a little taster of the knitting joy to come.

Casting on techniques

To get started with any project, you will first need to cast on to get the required number of stitches onto your needles. There are a number of different ways to do this explained here. There are also a number of ways to hold your yarn, so try them out to see which one works best for you.

Holding yarn

Winding yarn around your hand can help you maintain a consistent tension and make your knitting neater, quicker and easier. It is not a must – everyone has their own preferred way of working – but I've found it helps me.

There are two main ways of holding yarn: the 'English' way, in the right hand, or the 'continental' way, in the left hand. Both mean a slightly different way of knitting; many 'English' knitters who have switched to continental style say they find it quicker. If you're new to knitting, experiment with different holds to see which you prefer.

THE ENGLISH METHOD

1 Hold both needles in your left hand. Starting with the working yarn close to the needle, wind it once around the little finger of your right hand.

2 Thread it under the ring finger and middle finger, then up and over the index finger.

3 Take the right-hand needle in your right hand and you're ready to go. As you work, you will move your hand to bring the yarn around the needle. The movement is likely to grow less and less the more experienced you become – but everyone is different, so if you're moving a lot or not at all, don't worry. If it works, it works.

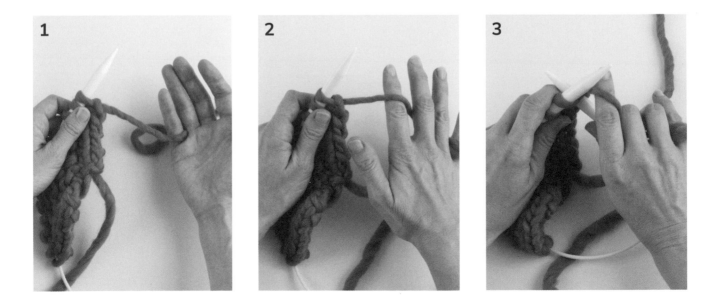

THE CONTINENTAL METHOD

1 Hold the needle you are about to work in your left hand. Starting with the working yarn close to the needle, wind it once around the little finger of your left hand.

2 Thread it under the ring finger and middle finger, then up and over the index finger.

3 Your right hand is free to pick up the right-hand needle and start working. Knitting in this way feels more like picking up the working yarn and pulling it through the stitch than winding it around the needle.

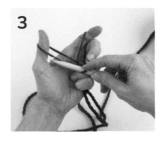

Long-tail cast on

The long-tail method is a stretchy cast on perfect for socks, hats, mittens and anything else that needs a bit of give.

1 Start with a long tail, leaving about 1in (2.5cm) for each stitch to be cast on. Make a slip knot and slip it onto a knitting needle.

2 With your left hand, create a slingshot shape: wrap the working yarn clockwise over your index finger, wrap the tail anticlockwise over your thumb and grasp the yarn ends in the remaining three fingers.

3 Use the needle tip to pick up the strand of yarn around the outside of your thumb, forming a loop.

4 Then pick up the strand of yarn on the inside of your index finger and pull it through the loop.

5 Let the yarn go and pull to tighten (not too tight). You now have two stitches cast on. Repeat steps 2–5 until you have cast on the required number of stitches.

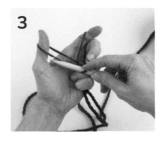

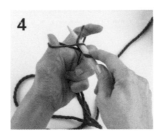

The knitted-on cast on

The knitted-on cast on is useful for beginners because it uses many of the same moves as the knit stitch, so you can practise before you even start knitting.

1   Start with your slip knot. Slip it onto your left-hand needle and tighten it to fit, but not so that it doesn't move easily along the needle.

2   Keeping your slip knot on the left-hand needle, insert your right-hand needle into the loop, from left to right, underneath the left-hand needle. (If it is tricky to do this, your slip knot is too tight – tug on the loop to loosen it.)

3   Bring the working yarn clockwise underneath the right-hand needle and back over the top, so you make a loop around it closer to the needle tips than the original slip knot. Use the tip of the right-hand needle to pull this new loop through the original slip knot.

4   Bring this new loop around to the tip of the left-hand needle and slip it on. You now have two stitches on the left-hand needle. To cast on more stitches, insert your right-hand needle into this new stitch and repeat steps 2–4. Repeat as many times as your pattern calls for.

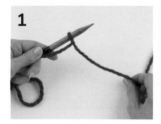

Garter stitch tab cast on

A garter stitch tab is a classic way to begin a shawl; it creates a neat band across the top of the work that can go from edge to edge uninterrupted.

1   Cast on three stitches and knit five rows. Note that there are three purl bumps along the side of the knitted tab.

2   Without turning the work, rotate the tab 90 degrees clockwise so the side is facing up. Insert your right-hand needle tip into the first purl bump and pick up a stitch. If this is tricky, it may be easier to pick up the purl bump with your left-hand needle and knit it as normal.

3   Repeat with the next two purl bumps. You should now have six stitches on your right-hand needle.

4   Turn the work 90 degrees clockwise again and pick up and knit three stitches along the cast-on edge. You now have nine stitches on your right-hand needle.

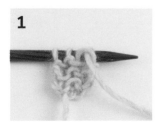
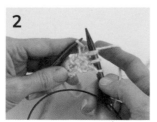
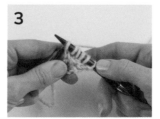
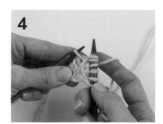

Judy's magic cast on

'Judy's magic cast on' was invented by Judy Becker, who introduced it on knitty.com. It is a great way to start toe-up socks and other projects with an invisible, seamless base – like the I Knit Anywhere project bag on page 74.

1 Hold two dpns (or the two tips of a circular needle if you're working with the magic loop method; see page 128) side by side. Leaving a long tail, make a slip knot and put it on the needle farther from you. This counts as your first stitch. Wrap the tail around your index finger and the working yarn around your thumb, as shown, and hold both ends in your remaining fingers.

2 Take the needle closer to you towards the yarn held by your index finger and wrap it around. It doesn't matter which way it wraps around the needle.

3 Now take the needle farther from you towards the yarn held by your thumb and wrap around. Again, it doesn't matter which way the yarn goes around the needle.

4 Repeat steps 2 and 3 until you have cast on the required number of stitches. On one side of the two rows of cast-on stitches there will be a little ridge. Make sure this ridge is facing up when you start knitting, so that it ends up on the inside of the sock.

5 To start knitting, hold the yarn tail tightly along the ridge of stitches. Before you start work, the last stitches to be cast on will feel quite loose. Before you work each stitch on this first round, check to see which leg is in front. If the rear leg of the stitch is in front of the front leg, knit the stitch through the back of the loop (see page 123). This means the stitch won't be twisted in the finished piece. When the front leg of the stitch is in front, knit the stitch as normal. The result is a seamless row of stitches from which you can work in the round, increasing as desired.

1

2
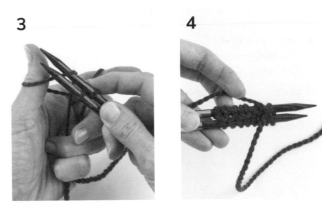

3

4

5

The knit and purl stitches

The knit and purl stitches are the building blocks of knitting. Once you know these stitches, you will be able to make nearly everything.

The knit stitch

This is your go-to, number-one stitch. If you can do the knit stitch, you can knit – it's that simple.

1 Hold the needle with stitches on in your left hand and insert the tip of the right-hand needle into the first stitch, underneath the left-hand needle. The needle goes through the stitch from left to right, even though the needle itself moves from right to left.

2 Take the working yarn underneath and back over the right-hand needle in a clockwise direction, creating a loop in front of the stitch that is holding both needles.

3 Use the tip of the right-hand needle to pull this loop through the original stitch.

4 The loop on your right-hand needle is the new stitch. Slip the original stitch off the end of the left-hand needle and let it fall. It now forms part of the fabric you are knitting.

5 Repeat steps 1–4 with the next stitch on the left-hand needle and then the following one until you have knitted every stitch. To knit the next row, simply turn the work around, take the right-hand needle – now with all the stitches on – in your left hand and start all over again.

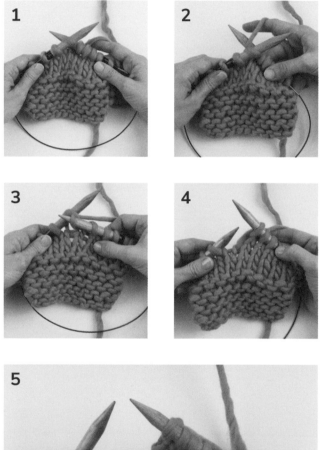

The purl stitch

The purl stitch is the mirror image of the knit stitch. Once you've mastered knit and purl, all the wonders of rib, moss stitch, cabling and all sorts of other textured stitches are yours for the taking.

1   Insert the tip of your right-hand needle into the front of the first stitch on the left-hand needle from right to left, with the right-hand needle above the left-hand needle.

2   Take the working yarn clockwise underneath the right-hand needle tip and back over it, creating a new loop in front of the stitch being worked.

3   Pull the right-hand needle tip back out of the stitch, taking the new loop of yarn with it. This is now the new stitch.

4   Let the original stitch slip off the left-hand needle to form part of the fabric.

5   Repeat steps 1–4 in the next stitch on the left-hand needle, and then the next, until all stitches have been purled. The fabric will look bobbly on the purled side and smoother on the knitted side. If you knit all the right-side rows and purl all the wrong-side rows, it is called stocking stitch, this is the most common stitch pattern you will see.

Working through the back loop

Working through the back loop twists a stitch. This can be used simply for the visual effect, or to avoid a hole – for example, when increasing.

1   Each stitch has two legs straddling the needle. The one closest to you is the front leg; the farther one is the back leg. To knit through the back loop, insert the tip of the right-hand needle into the back loop instead of the front. Knit this stitch as normal.

2   You can purl through the back loop in the same way.

Shaping your work

To make your knitting fit better – and look more interesting – the fabric sometimes needs to be shaped by increasing or decreasing the number of stitches. There are lots of ways to do this; here are some popular methods for both increasing and decreasing.

Knit front and back

Before you begin, take a look at the first stitch on your left-hand needle. The front of the loop (on the side of the needle facing you) should be a little in front of the back of the loop. These are also known as the front and back legs of the stitch.

1   Start off by knitting the first stitch through its front loop as normal, but do not slip the stitch off the end of the left-hand needle.

2   Keeping the original stitch on the left-hand needle and the new stitch on the right-hand needle, take the right-hand needle tip to the back of the left-hand needle and insert it into the back loop of the original stitch.

3   Wrap the yarn around and pull the new loop through as you would in the knit stitch, then slip the original stitch off the end of the left-hand needle. You now have two stitches on the right-hand needle knitted from just one stitch on the left-hand needle. If you work this increase at each end of the row, your fabric will get wider.

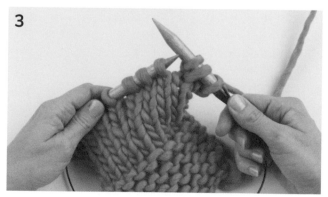

Yarn overs

Yarn overs can be used for a simple increase, or to create a decorative hole in your knitting. They are the basis of all lace knitting. Once you can increase using yarn overs and master some decreases, you will be surprised how many complicated-looking lace patterns become possible.

1   Knit the first stitch as normal, then bring the yarn to the front of the work.

2   Knit the next stitch as normal, taking the yarn over the top of the right-hand needle to the back of the work. This will create a new loop in the next row of knitting.

3   You now have two options. If you work the next row as normal – in this case, a purl row – you will end up with an increase that has created a little hole where the yarn over was.

4   To avoid these holes, when you come to the stitches created by the yarn overs on the next row, work them through the back loop (as in knitting front and back, opposite), but in this case purling through the back loop. The result is a neat fabric without any holes.

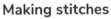

Making stitches

Making a new stitch usually means picking up the bar between the stitch just worked and the next one onto your left-hand needle and working it either through the front or back loop, to create a slanted increase. Make one left (m1L) is usually done at the beginning of a row to create a right-slanted increase, whereas make one right (m1R) creates a left-slanted increase at the end of a row.

MAKE ONE LEFT

1   Knit the first stitch on the needle, then look for the bar that sits between this stitch and the next on the left-hand needle. Insert the tip of the right-hand needle from front to back through this bar, pick it up and slip it onto the tip of the left-hand needle.

2   Knit this new stitch through the back loop.

MAKE ONE RIGHT

These increases create neatly slanted shaping at each side of the fabric.

1 Knit to the last stitch on the left-hand needle, then look for the bar between this stitch and the last stitch on the right-hand needle. Insert the tip of the right-hand needle from back to front into this bar, pick it up and slip it onto the tip of the left-hand needle.

2 Knit this stitch through the front loop as normal.

Knit two together

Knit two together (k2tog) is the simplest and most common decrease and creates a right-leaning stitch. You can purl two together in a similar way, simply by purling instead of knitting.

1 Instead of inserting your needle into just one stitch, insert it into the next two stitches on the left-hand needle, just as if you were going to knit a single stitch. Wrap the working yarn around the needle and pull the new loop through the original two stitches.

2 Slip them off the end of the left-hand needle, just as you would if you were knitting a single stitch. You have now made two stitches into one stitch.

Slip, slip, knit

Slip, slip, knit (ssk) is a way to make a left-leaning decrease.

1   Insert the tip of the right-hand needle into the next stitch on the left-hand needle as if to knit it, but instead just slip it from the left-hand needle to the right-hand needle.

2   Repeat with the next stitch so you have two slipped stitches on the right-hand needle. Insert the left-hand needle through both those stitches from left to right on top of the right-hand needle. Wrap the working yarn around the right-hand needle, knitting the two slipped stitches together through the back loop, and slip them off the end of the left-hand needle.

Slip one, knit one, pass slipped stitch over

Slip one, knit one, pass slipped stitch over, or skpo, is another common left-leaning decrease.

1   Insert the tip of the right-hand needle into the next stitch on the left-hand needle as if you were about to knit it, but instead slip it to the right-hand needle.

2   Knit the next stitch as normal.

3   Use the tip of the left-hand needle to pick up the slipped stitch – now the second-to-last stitch on the right hand-needle – and pass it over the knitted stitch, the last stitch on the right-hand needle.

4   You can see a pronounced left-leaning decrease.

Knitting in the round

Some knitters are intimidated by the idea of knitting in the round, whereas others love it – especially because it means you can knit stocking stitch without having to do purl rows. Knitting in the round is perfect for making hats, gloves, socks and cowls.

The magic loop method

There are several ways to knit in the round: you can use a number of double-pointed needles or a circular needle exactly the right size for your knit. The magic loop method is handy because you can use the same circular needle for any size of knitting. It is simpler than it looks – once you've got going, you're sure to love it.

1 Cast on the number of stitches you want and slide them onto the connecting cable of your circular needle.

2 Find the middle of the stitches and pull the cable out through this point – but not so far that any stitches drop off the ends of the needle tips.

3 Leave the half of the stitches connected to the working yarn on the cable – these will be known as the back stitches. Slide the other half of the stitches onto the left-hand needle tip. These are the front stitches.

4 Bring the right-hand needle tip around and knit the first stitch on the left-hand needle tip. Pull the working yarn tightly afterwards; you will find your stitches have joined in a loop. It is a good idea to place a marker at this point so that you know where your round begins and ends.

5 Carry on knitting until you have worked all the front stitches. Taking care not to turn the stitches you have worked upside down or inside out, turn the work around so that the stitches you have just knitted are now sitting at the back on the left-hand needle tip and the cast-on stitches are at the front on the cable.

6 Pull the cable until the cast-on stitches now at the front of the work are sitting on the needle tip in front of the other needle tip. This is now your left-hand needle. Take care not to drop any stitches at this point. Pull the needle tip at the back out of the back stitches so that they now sit on the cable. This is now your right-hand needle tip. Bring this needle tip around and work the first stitch on the left-hand needle. Carry on knitting until you have worked all the stitches on the needle tip. You have now knitted one round. Repeat for as many rounds as you like, creating a neat tube of knitting.

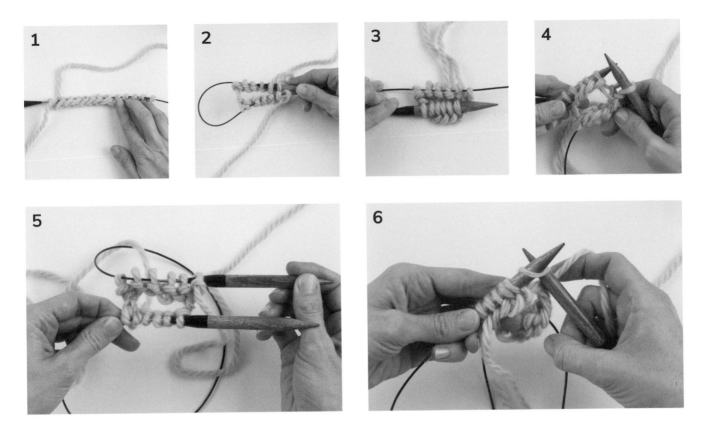

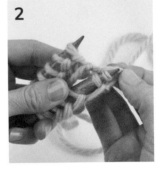

The jogless join

Sometimes, joining in the round can leave a gap or irregularity that needs to be patched up with duplicate stitch. This simple trick is a way to avoid that and create a really neat join.

1 Cast on one more stitch than you need. Once the stitches have been distributed across your needles, slip the last cast-on stitch onto the first needle.

2 Use your fingers or a needle tip to pass the first cast-on stitch over the last cast-on stitch.

3 Now return the last cast-on stitch to its original needle. The result is a really neat, tight join.

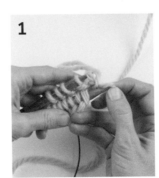

Cables

Cable patterns can seem daunting, mainly because the cable abbreviations look so complicated at first glance. In fact, working cables is as simple as knitting and purling, and each abbreviation, once expanded, gives you clear instructions telling you exactly what to do. Here are a couple of basic cables. Once you have the hang of these, you will be able to work any cable by simply following the instructions in the individual pattern.

Cable four front (C4F)

1 Slip the next two stitches to a cable needle held at the front of the work.

2 Leaving these two stitches, knit the following two stitches as normal.

3 Now knit the two stitches on the cable needle.

4 You have created a left-leaning twist.

Cable four back (C4B)

1 Slip the next two stitches to a cable needle held at the back of the work.

2 Leaving these two stitches, knit the following two stitches as normal.

3 Now knit the two stitches on the cable needle.

4 You have created a right-leaning twist.

TIP: Stick one end of the cable needle into the knitted fabric below the bit you're working on to hold it in place and stop stitches slipping off.

131

Fairisle or stranded knitting

Some patterns call for you to work more than one colour in the same row. In this book we strand the colour not in use behind the colour being worked in a technique sometimes known as Fairisle, after Fair Isle in Shetland, Scotland, which is famous for colourful knits using this technique.

Holding yarn for colourwork knitting

There are two ways to hold multiple yarns when working colourwork:

- TWO-HANDED: hold one yarn in the 'English' style in your right hand and the other in the 'continental' style in your left.

- ONE-HANDED: wind the different yarns around the same hand and pick the one you want when it comes to each stitch. You can buy knitting 'thimbles' that help keep yarns organized when working in this way.

Working stranded colourwork

Most colourwork patterns are set out in a chart. Each different-coloured square represents a different stitch.

1 Work the required number of stitches in the first colour.
2 Then work the required number of stitches in the second colour.
3 The yarn not in use is stranded at the back of the fabric. To avoid long strands that may get caught on things or pull on the fabric if they end up being too tight, you need to catch the yarn not in use at regular intervals. I would recommend doing this every two or three stitches. This also helps to keep your tension even. To catch the yarn not in use, simply lift it up and take the working yarn across it as you work the next stitch.
4 This will secure it at the back of the fabric...
5 ...but won't show through at the front.

TIP: When working stranded colourwork, you may find that your tension is different from your standard stocking-stitch tension. In this case, try to consciously knit more loosely or tightly, or change your needle size to compensate.

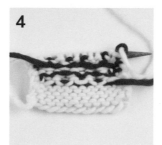
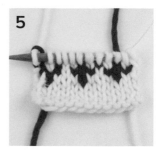

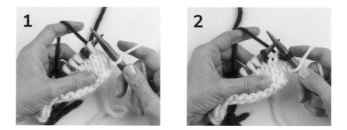

Brioche knitting

Brioche knitting is widely reputed to be challenging, but in fact is one of the simplest and most pleasing techniques I've encountered. Using slipped stitches worked together on the next row, it creates a squashy, reversible ribbed fabric and a wonderful colour effect when worked in two shades. Brioche also has a wonderful rhythm that is perfect for knitters who want their craft to be about relaxation and wellbeing.

One-colour brioche worked flat

1   Brioche starts with a set-up row. The order of knitted and slipped stitches will vary from pattern to pattern; in this case, we will start with a simple knit stitch. *Bring the yarn to the front of the work.

2   Slip the next stitch purlwise, still holding the yarn at the front of the work.

3   Knit the next stitch as normal, creating a yarn over across the slipped stitch. Repeat from * to the end of the row, or as your pattern directs.

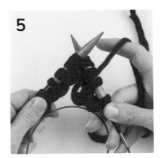

4   On the next row, you will see ordinary knit stitches alternating with slipped stitches with a yarn over. As you come to each knit stitch, bring the yarn to the front, then slip the stitch purlwise, as in step 2. This is known as slip one, yarn over (sl1yo).

5   The next stitch is a slipped stitch with a yarn over across it. Knit the slipped stitch together with its yarn over. This is called brioche knit 1, or brk1. It will also create a yarn over across the stitch you just slipped.

6   Continue to work in this way until you are directed otherwise by your pattern. Each row is worked in the same way, regardless of whether it is a RS or a WS row. The result is a reversible ribbed fabric.

Two-colour brioche worked flat

Two-colour brioche has to be worked on a circular or double-pointed needle. Work a set-up row and a single row of (sl1yo, brk1) in colour A, just as you would in one-colour brioche.

1   At the end of the row, do not turn the work but slide the stitches back to the other end of the needle to work this side again.

2   Join B and purl the first stitch together with its yarn over. This is known as brioche purl 1, or brp1.

3   Slip the next stitch purlwise.

4   Take the yarn over the top of the needles to the back of the work, then back to the front of the work between the needles to create the yarn over across the slipped stitch.

5   The yarn is now at the front, ready to work the next brp stitch. Continue in this way to the end of the row, then turn the work.

6   On the next row use A to work a row of (brp1, sl1yo), as you did on the previous row with B. At the end of the row, do not turn the work but slide the stitches back to the other end to work that side again.

7   Now use B to work a row of (sl1yo, brk1). At the end of the row, turn the work.

8   These four rows form two-colour brioche and are repeated. The result is a reversible two-colour ribbed fabric with A dominant on one side...

9   ...and B dominant on the other side.

One-colour brioche in the round

1   Join your work in the round and work a set-up round of (k1, sl1yo) around.

2   Once back at the beginning of the round, the first stitch will be a single stitch without a yarn over, so work (sl1yo, brk1) around.

3   When you come back to the start of the round, you will find a slipped stitch with a yarn over. This time, work (brp1, sl1yo) around.

4   These two rows are repeated to work brioche in the round.

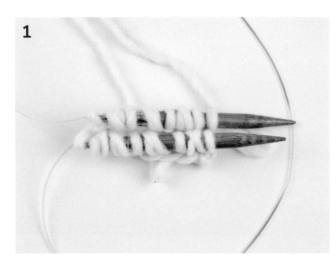

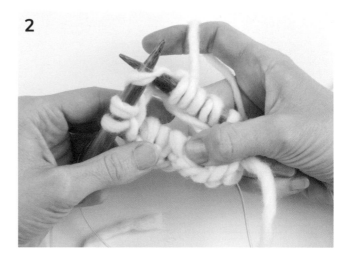

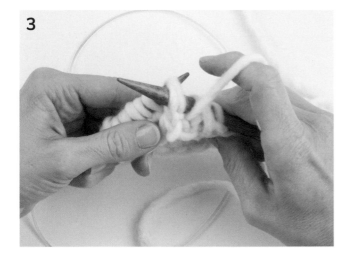

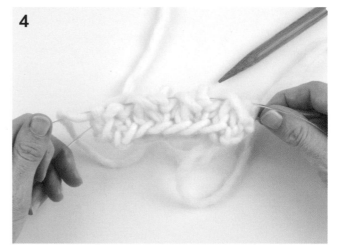

Two-colour brioche in the round

If you've never tried brioche before, this is a great way to start. It introduces you to all the basics of brioche knitting, but is actually simpler than two-colour brioche knitted flat. Once you've got the hang of it in the round, you'll have no trouble with the flat version.

1   Cast on with A and join in the round, then work a set-up round of (sl1yo, k1). The next round is worked in B. Leaving A hanging at the back of the work, join B at the back of the work but bring it to the front to work the first stitch, which is a sl1yo.

2   Using B work brp1, purling the stitch together with its yarn over. Continue to work (sl1yo, brp1) around.

3   The next round is worked in A. Work (sl1yo, brk1) around. These two rounds are repeated. The result is a lovely two-colour rib effect, with A dominant on one side and B on the other.

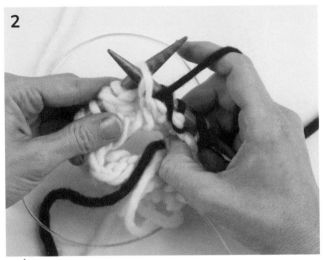

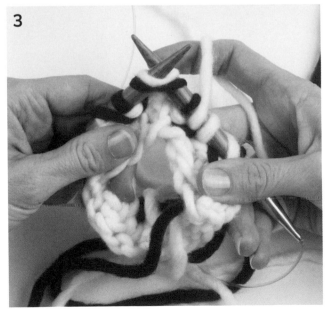

Useful techniques

Once you know the basics of knitting, there are a few useful techniques to pick up to help you make more advanced pieces with a professional-looking finish.

Kitchener stitch

Kitchener stitch is a neat way of joining two sets of live stitches with an invisible seam, giving a neat finish.

1 Hold your two pieces with the wrong sides together and needle tips facing to the right. You must have the same number of stitches on each needle. If you have left a long tail for sewing up, thread that onto a tapestry needle. If not, use a length of the same yarn as you have used for the rest of the project.

2 First set-up step: insert the tapestry needle into the first stitch on the front needle, as if to purl. Pull the yarn through, but do not slip the stitch off the needle.

3 Second set-up step: insert the tapestry needle into the first stitch on the back needle, as if to knit. Again, leave this stitch on the needle.

4 Now we are ready to start grafting. Insert the tapestry needle into the first stitch on the front needle, as if to knit. This time, slip the stitch off the needle as you pull the yarn through.

5 Insert the tapestry needle into what was the second stitch on the front needle but is now the first, as if to purl and pull yarn through, but do not slip the stitch off the needle.

6 Insert the tapestry needle into the first stitch on the back needle and slip that stitch off the needle.

7 Now insert the tapestry needle into what was the second stitch on the back needle but is now the first and pull yarn through, but do not slip that stitch off the needle.

8 Repeat steps 4–7 until two stitches remain, one on each needle, then work steps 4 and 6 in these last stitches.

9 You now have a row of stitches joining the two pieces of fabric. They may be a little loose. Use the tip of the tapestry needle to work along the row, gently tightening each stitch. Finally, you have a neat row of stitches making a seamless join.

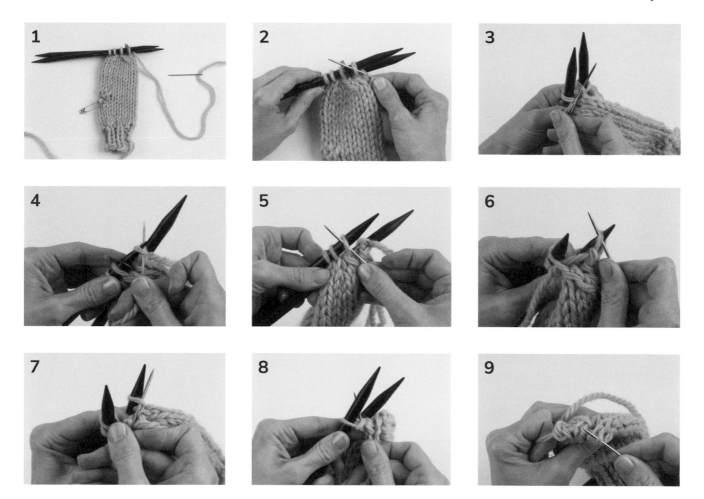

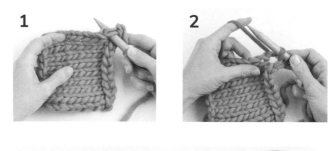

Picking up stitches

Picking up stitches from the edge of knitting is great for adding on neat finishing bands and a way to avoid sewing.

1   With the right side of the fabric facing you and starting in the bottom right-hand corner, *insert the tip of your left-hand needle into the fabric.

2   Pull a loop of working yarn through this hole to create a stitch on your left-hand needle.

3   Repeat from * as directed by your pattern. You can now work these picked-up stitches just like normal stitches.

Shadow-wrap short rows

There are a number of ways to work the 'wrap and turn' used to avoid holes when shaping fabric using short rows. My favourite is the shadow-wrap method, invented by *Socktopus* author Alice Yu; this is very neat and less fiddly than some other methods.

1   Work up to the point where you are asked to wrap and turn in your pattern, then knit the stitch to be wrapped. Underneath this stitch you will notice the stitch that came before it – Alice calls this the 'mama' stitch, while the stitch on the needle is the 'daughter' stitch.

2   Lift the mama stitch onto the left-hand needle, taking care not to twist it, then knit it and drop it off the left-hand needle.

3   You now have two stitches on the right-hand needle, both coming out of the same mama stitch – the daughter stitch and the 'shadow' stitch. Next time you come to these two stitches, you will work them together as if they were one stitch.

4   To work a shadow wrap purlwise, work to the stitch to be wrapped, then slip it purlwise onto the right-hand needle.

5   Lift the mama stitch of the slipped stitch onto the left-hand needle, being careful not to twist it, then purl it and drop the mama stitch off the needle. Once again, you have a daughter stitch and a shadow stitch coming out of the same mama stitch. When you come to these stitches again, work them as if they were one stitch.

Casting off

To finish a piece of knitting, you will need to cast off all your stitches, tying them up so that nothing comes unravelled. There are a number of ways to do this.

Standard cast off

This is the most commonly used cast-off technique.

1   Start by working the first two stitches as normal: if it is a knit stitch, knit it; if a purl stitch, purl it unless your pattern says otherwise.

2   Use the tip of your left-hand needle to lift the first stitch on the right-hand needle up and over the top of the second stitch and off the end of the right-hand needle. This stitch is now cast off.

3   Knit the next stitch on the left-hand needle so that you again have two stitches on the right-hand needle, then repeat step 2.

4   Keep repeating step 3 until you have one stitch left on the right-hand needle and none on the left-hand needle. Pass the rest of the ball, or the end of the working yarn, through this last stitch, using your fingers to make the stitch big enough for the ball to fit through, then pull tightly on the working yarn. You should have a neat and tidy row of cast-off stitches.

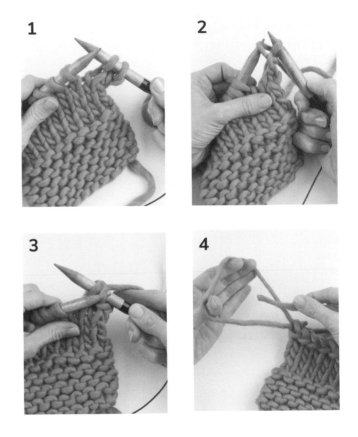

Three-needle cast off

This technique not only casts off the live stitches but also joins them together seamlessly, so there is no need to sew two edges together.

Start with your live stitches on two knitting needles held parallel to each other in your left hand, with right sides together so the seam will appear on the wrong side.

With a third needle held in your right hand, insert the tip into the first stitch on both left-hand needles at the same time and knit them together. Repeat with the second stitch on both left-hand needles, then pass the first stitch on the right-hand needle over the second. Repeat these steps until a single stitch remains, then fasten off.

Crochet techniques

Crochet is a little different from knitting – it uses a hook and has only one live stitch at a time instead of a number of them. Basic crochet is very straightforward and can be a great way to finish or edge your knits.

Slip stitch

1 Insert the hook into the next st and bring the yarn over the needle.

2 Pull the yarn through both loops on the hook, joining them (1 loop on hook).

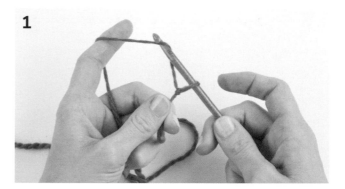

Chain stitch

1 Start with a slip knot on your hook and bring the yarn over the hook...

2 ...then pull it through the slip knot to create a second loop.

3 Repeat steps 1 and 2 until your chain is the required length.

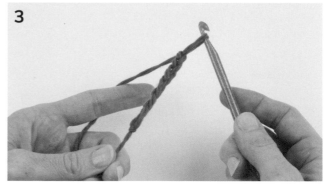

Double crochet

1 Insert the hook through the next loop and bring the yarn over the hook, then pull it through the first loop on the hook only.

2 Now bring the yarn over the hook again and pull it through both loops now on the hook.

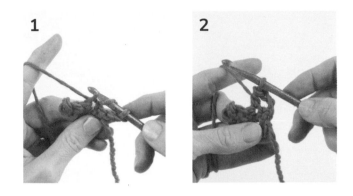

Half treble crochet

1   Bring the yarn over the hook, then insert the hook into the next st, bring the yarn over the hook again and pull it through the first st (3 loops on hook).

2 Bring the yarn over again and pull it through all three loops (1 loop on hook).

Finishing techniques

There are a number of techniques that you will need to know in order to finish off your projects neatly, including sewing pieces together, blocking to size and weaving in ends. Here we also explain some decorative techniques, including Swiss darning and making pompoms to add a unique finishing touch to a handmade item.

Weaving in ends

This technique creates a neat finish without reducing the elasticity of the knit.

1 When you come to the end of a project, you'll have a number of ends waiting to be woven in on the wrong side of the work. Choose a large-eyed tapestry needle – blunt or sharp tips should work equally well. With the wrong side facing (in the case of a stocking stitch project, that's the purl side), thread a yarn end through the eye of the needle. The back of the work is made up of a series of curved stitches: I will call them bowls (which dip downwards) and hats (which curve upwards). Starting with the stitch next to your loose end, insert your needle first underneath the hat next to it, then, following the stitch already running through those loops, upwards through the bowl above it on the right-hand side. Miss out the next hat, upwards and to the left of your working yarn.

2 Insert the needle downwards and to the right into the next bowl to the left of your working yarn, and then through the hat beneath and to the right of it.

3 Miss out the next bowl, then insert your needle upwards and to the right, as in step 1.

4 Repeat steps 1–3 until you have a row of stitches duplicating the stitches in the knitting and neatly securing the loose end. Keep checking that your stitches aren't showing on the right side of the work.

5 Your weaving should be completely invisible on the right side, and the fabric remains nice and stretchy.

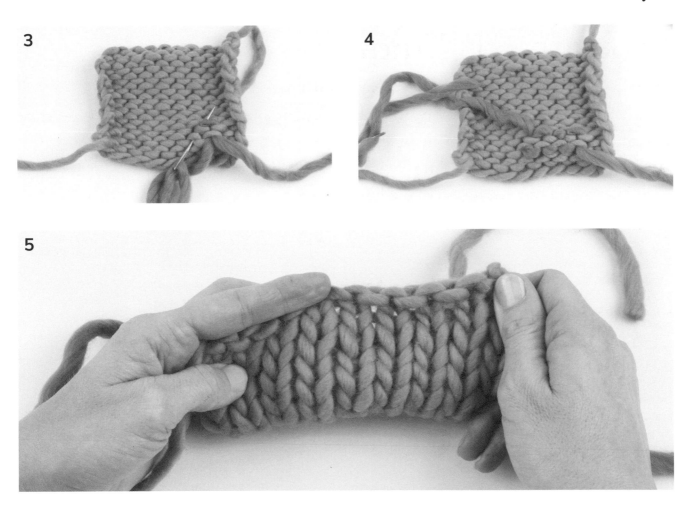

Blocking

The main aim in blocking is to use water to relax knitted stitches, even out irregularities and encourage the garment into the shape and size it was intended to be. As knits tend to be stretchy, they can be obliging.

If you feel the need to really stretch out your knit, you could give it a gentle hand-wash in cool water with a special wool wash. Squeeze out the excess water but do not wring, then roll up the garment in a clean towel and tread on it. This will gently remove the rest of the excess water (it's also a good approach when hand-washing your knits further down the line).

Pin the garment out to the measurements required. Many blocking mats come handily marked with measurements. If you don't have this specialist equipment, you can lay out clean towels on a bed or carpet (over a waterproof cover if the garment is still very wet) and use a measuring tape. Make sure the pins you use are rust proof, and use enough pins so you get a straight edge along your knitting. Blocking wires can help you achieve this.

I don't usually wet-block my designs unless they need particular stretching. My preferred method, and the one I have used for all of the designs in this book, is to lay the garment on top of a couple of towels either on my bed or on the floor, pin it to the correct measurements, sprinkle it with a small amount of water, spray it with a blocking spray (I use Flatter from Soak), then cover it with damp cloths. I the muslin cloths I used to swaddle my kids when they were babies, but tea towels are fine, too.

In either case, leave the garment pinned in place until it is completely dry. It makes a considerable difference to the finish, so I recommend you try it.

Joining pieces with mattress stitch

Some knits only need a couple of ends weaving in and they're good to go, but others will need different pieces of knitted fabric to be sewn together. Mattress stitch is a good technique to create a neat join.

1   Start with your two finished pieces next to each other, right sides up. Thread a large-eyed, blunt-ended needle with a long piece of yarn. Normally you would use the same yarn you knitted with and could even use a yarn tail; in this case, I used a contrasting yarn so it shows up better.

2   Insert the needle tip into the stitch at the very left edge of the right-hand fabric from the right side to the wrong side, take it under two bars of stitches and bring it back through the right side and pull through.

3   Repeat step 2 on the left-hand fabric. Move back to the right-hand fabric and repeat step 2 with the next two stitches up. Then do the same with the corresponding stitches on the left-hand side.

4   Pull the yarn through and tighten it. You now have a neat join that is almost invisible on the right side...

5   ...and a neat seam is showing on the wrong side.

146

Swiss darning or duplicate stitch

Swiss darning, or duplicate stitch, is a way of embroidering your knitted fabric almost invisibly by following exactly the lines of the stitch you are sewing over.

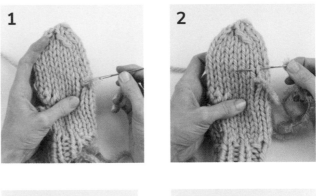

1   Thread a length of the yarn you're using to embroider onto a large-eyed, blunt-ended yarn needle. Bring this needle up through the bottom point of the V of the knit stitch you want to cover.

2   Take the yarn up and to the right, then thread the needle from right to left behind the point of the V above this stitch.

3   Pull the yarn through, then take the needle to the back of the work at the same point at which you first brought it to the front.

4   The stitch is completely covered. Repeat steps 1–3 as directed by your pattern.

Making pompoms

Pompoms are a great way to finish off hats, scarves and all sorts of other items. They are easy to make: you can either use a pompom maker or two thick rings of card. To make the card rings, draw a circle around the size you want your pompom to be on a piece of card, then draw a smaller circle in the middle. Cut out both of these circles to form a ring, then repeat so you have two rings.

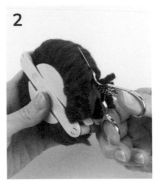

1   Wind your yarn evenly all around your pompom maker or both card rings held together until the central hole is full. You don't need to pull it too tightly.

2   Use scissors to cut the yarn all around the edge of the outer circle.

3   Pull the two rings or the two sides of the pompom maker apart slightly and tie a length of yarn tightly around the middle. You may want to leave a long length of yarn for sewing.

4   Now remove the pompom maker and trim to size.

Abbreviations

alt	alternative
beg	begin/ning
brk1	brioche knit 1: knit together the slipped stitch from the previous row with the yarn over across it
brp1	brioche purl 1: purl together the slipped stitch from the previous row with the yarn over across it
ch	chain
cm	centimetre/s
cn	cable needle
cont	continue
dc	double crochet
dec	decrease
dpn(s)	double-pointed needle(s)
foll	follows/following
g	gramme/s
g st	garter stitch (every row knit)
htr	half treble crochet
in	inch/es
inc	increase
k	knit
k2tog	knit two stitches together (decrease 1)
k3tog	knit three stitches together (decrease 2)
kfb	knit into front and back of next stitch (increase 1)
kwise	knitwise
LH	left hand
m	marker
m1	make 1 stitch: pick up the loop lying between the two stitches and knit into the back of it (increase 1)
m1L	make one left-leaning stitch (increase 1)
m1R	make one right-leaning stitch (increase 1)
m1p	make 1 purlwise
mm	millimetre/s
m st	moss stitch
p	purl
p2tog	purl two stitches together (decrease 1)
p3tog	purl three stitches together (decrease 2)
patt	pattern
pm	place marker
psso	pass slipped stitch over
pwise	purlwise
rem	remain/ing
rep	repeat
rev st st	reverse stocking stitch (RS purl, WS knit)
RH	right hand
rnd	round
RS	right side
skpo	slip one, knit one, pass the slipped stitch over (decrease 1)
sk2po	slip one, knit two together, pass slipped stitch over (decrease 2)
s2kpo	slip two stitches one at a time knitwise, knit one, pass two slipped stitches over (decrease 2)
sp2po	slip one purlwise, purl two together, pass slipped stitch over (decrease 2)
sl1	slip one stitch
sl1p	slip one stitch purlwise
sl1yo	bring yarn to the front, slip next st pwise, work following stitch as directed creating a yarn over across the slipped stitch
sm	slip marker
ssk	slip next two stitches one at a time knitwise to right-hand needle, insert tip of left-hand needle through both stitches and knit them together (decrease 1)
st(s)	stitch(es)
st st	stocking stitch
tbl	through back loop
tog	together
w&t	wrap and turn
WS	wrong side
wyib	with yarn at the back
wyif	with yarn at the front
yf	yarn forward
yo	yarn over

Conversions

The patterns in this book use UK terms for both knitting and crochet terms. Below are some translations for crafters who might be more familiar with US terms, which are sometimes different. We also include conversion tables for knitting needle and crochet hook sizes.

Knitting needle sizes

METRIC	UK	US
4.5mm	7	7
5mm	6	8
6mm	4	10
6.5mm	3	10½
7mm	2	10½
8mm	0	11
9mm	00	13
10mm	000	15
12mm	–	17
15mm	–	19
25mm	–	50

Crochet hook sizes

METRIC	UK	US
2mm	14	–
2.25mm	13	B/1
2.5mm	12	–
2.75mm	–	C/2
3mm	11	–
3.25mm	10	D/3
3.5mm	9	E/4
3.75mm	–	F/5
4mm	8	G/6
4.5mm	7	7
5mm	6	H/8
5.5mm	5	I/9
6mm	4	J/10
6.5mm	3	K/10½

Crochet terms

UK	US
dc (double crochet)	sc (single crochet)
htr (half treble)	hdc (half double crochet)
tr (treble crochet)	dc (double crochet)

Knitting terms

US	US
cast off	bind off
moss stitch	seed stitch
stocking stitch	stockinette stitch

746.432
BOG

Suppliers

Baa Ram Ewe
baaramewe.co.uk

Cascade Yarns
cascadeyarns.com

Erika Knight
erikaknight.co.uk

Knit Pro
knitpro.eu

Loopy Mango
loopymango.com

Malabrigo
malabrigoyarn.com

Rico
rico-design.de

Rowan
knitrowan.com

West Yorkshire Spinners
wyspinners.com

Wool and the Gang
woolandthegang.com

Rainbow ribbons by Berisfords
To find your stockist, email
groves@stockistenquiries.co.uk.

Acknowledgements

I am very much indebted to the wonderful yarn producers who supplied me with the beautiful materials to knit these designs; not just for the yarn itself, but also for their moral support, enthusiasm and inspiration.

The very helpful staff at Kerrie Berrie Beads & Jewellery in Brighton (kerrieberrie.co.uk) gave me a free crash course in jewellery making that led to some very happy hours creating pretty stitch markers. Many of the buttons and other bits and pieces came from The Stitchery in Lewes, East Sussex (the-stitchery.co.uk), where the staff are always friendly and helpful.

I would not have got very far in my knitting without the friendly and supportive advice of craft gurus and brilliant designers Jo Allport, Jeanette Sloan and Sarah Hazell. I could not have finished this book without the help and support of the world's loveliest technical editor, Rachel Vowles, and my awesome assistant Abby Costen. I'm also very grateful to my other colleagues and employers at GMC and my fantastic photographer, Laurel Guilfoyle, who makes everything look great.

Much thanks and love go to my gorgeous family, who put up with a lot while I was writing this book. It would not have been possible without their love and support and I hope one day to be able to pay them back with knitted goods.

GMC Publications would like to thank:
Grace and Jonathan from MOT Models, Stanley and Daisy Richardson; Lindsey Poole for hair and make-up; The Old Forge, South Heighton for letting us shoot in their home and garden. KnitPro for providing the petal shawl stick pictured on pages 20 and 23.

Picture credits

Index

To order a book, or to request a catalogue, contact:
GMC Publications Ltd, Castle Place,
166 High Street, Lewes, East Sussex,
BN7 1XU, United Kingdom
Tel: +44 (0)1273 488005
www.gmcbooks.com